MW01136630

Restoring the *Integrity* of His Name: JESUS

Attitudes & Habits of a Godly Perspective

DARRYL SMITH

TABLE OF CONTENTS

PREFACE

Some of the material in this book may be controversial to some Christians based on their religious and denominational teachings and beliefs, but the contents of this book represent those things God has inspired me through the Holy Spirit to write.

The passion and purpose of this writing is spun out of the leading of the Holy Spirit to the Christian community and believers in the Lord Jesus Christ who have been given the responsibility of defending and upholding the integrity of the greatest name given among men. The world, even the church institution, seems to have ignored, overlooked, minimized, or simply taken for granted that God transformed Himself to be the most influential and significant entity to walk the earth in the person of *Jesus Christ*.

In this current era, it is not unusual or uncommon to watch popular television programs that are considered acceptable for family viewing of all ages and hear one of the actors say something derogatory with Jesus' name mentioned in it. Neither is it an unusual occurrence to be in a public place such as a shopping mall, a bus stop, a college campus, a sporting event, or some place where people socially gather, and hear someone use a phrase with the name Jesus in a manner that brings great disrespect to God and to those who honor and reverence that name. I suppose this can be expected of those who don't know the Son of God. It pains and saddens many Christians to hear anyone use the name of Jesus in a joking, jesting, or foolish manner.

I was inspired to write this book when I began pastoring a small rural denominational church in 2006. As I was getting acclimated to what God had called me to do, and as I diligently sought His face through prayer to better acquaint myself with His will, I heard God say to me, "Restore the integrity of My name." At first it seemed like the wrong theme for a church ministry because it is often assumed that believers already give God the highest name regard, but as time progressed, I realized why God had given me this ministry theme. I began to see from God's perspective how the name of Jesus had become entrapped in nonsensical and false representation, even among confessing believers, and how the life and message of Christ is being expressed through religious jargons, dogmas, rhetoric, and activities that vaguely emphasizes His true holiness. It is not only the verbal dishonoring of His name by the unsaved that is troubling, it is also how Christians conduct church business, live their personal lives, perform professional services, and engage in other behaviors and activities as Christians where applications of integrity are essential, but often lacking. In some professions, it is not uncommon to see work trucks, vans, and other business signage advertising and promoting a business as Christian owned and operated, but when doing business with poor quality and dishonest business practices, the nameplate as Christian owned and operated becomes disreputable as a business of integrity. There have been multiple public incidents where the name of Jesus has been mischaracterized through the behavior of some who confess Him as Lord, particularly love. For example, when a Christian condemns the unbelieving, the wrong message is communicated because the believer has forgotten that they too had to be forgiven for sins. The woman who was brought to Jesus as the result of being caught in adultery by her accusers was told by Jesus that he did not condemn her, but she should sin no more (John 8:3-11).

The misbehavior in handling ministry finances for which church leaders have been indicted and imprisoned, and their personal misconduct, should be addressed as serious breaches of integrity of the name of Jesus Christ. The accounts of sexual misconduct and abuse by members of clergy have created a cloud of shame and loss of respect, and diminishes what the church is to represent to the world.

In our modern culture, it appears that the true meaning of worship of God has been replaced with theatrical and entertainment pleasures where people with their gifts and talents are celebrated more than the person of Jesus Christ. Throughout this writing, I will be discussing various applications of restoring the integrity of His name.

During the early part of 2015, while fasting and consecrating myself to the Lord, I was again reminded to write concerning integrity in the church, but with a greater emphasis of exposing the writing to a broader Christian audience. God instructed me to use Isaiah 58:12 as the supporting theme in delivering this message:

> And they that shall be of thee shall build the old waste places: thou shalt raise up the foundations of many generations; and thou shalt be called, The repairer of the breach, The restorer of paths to dwell in.

I am humbled to have been chosen by God to announce, publish, broadcast, and participate with a larger network of believers set apart to this mandate of lifting the message of restoring the integrity of His name. *It must be clear that the title of this book does not in any way indicate that the name of Jesus itself has lost virtue, integrity, or power.* The church and believers in general have diminished Christ in many applications of personal life and public ministry, and this is a trumpet-sounding message to return to the manner of living that God intended for the church.

Many religious institutions and churches have bishops, pastors, and overseers who are the voices of conscience to those who believe in Christ and support their ministries. Therefore, these voices should be universally consistent with the voice of the Holy Spirit and the Word of God. There are some church leaders who have lifted themselves to become the object of attention and adoration, and in the worst case, the object of worship. This has become an accepted behavior in so many Christian churches.

CHAPTER ONE

Who is Jesus Christ?

The exact year and date of Jesus' birth is unknown, but according to Scripture, He was born in Bethlehem of Judea in the days of Herod the king, whose reign spanned from 37 to 4 BCE (Before the Common or Current Era). Before his birth, an angel appeared in a dream to Joseph, who was engaged to marry the virgin Mary, and revealed to him that the child she was carrying was of the Holy Ghost, told him not to fear taking Mary as his wife, and stated that the child would be named Jesus.

The prophet Isaiah prophesized of the birth of Jesus. In Isaiah 9:6 it is recorded:

> For unto us a child is born, unto us a son is given: and the government shall be upon his shoulder: and his name shall be called Wonderful, Counsellor, The mighty God, The everlasting Father, The Prince of Peace.

Afterwards, Joseph took Mary to be his wife as the angel had instructed him. Soon after Jesus' birth, and following a warning by an angel about Herod's desire to kill Jesus, Joseph and Mary took their child and went into Egypt. After Herod's death, an angel appeared to Joseph again and said, "Go into the land of Israel," but since Herod's son reigned in Judaea, this caused some safety concerns for Joseph and his family. Subsequently, God gave Joseph another warning in a dream, so Joseph moved to Nazareth in Galilee, where Jesus grew up as a child. (Matthew 1:20-21; Matthew 2:13-23; Isaiah 7:14).

It is important to highlight the purpose of Jesus coming into the world: to redeem or save people from the penalty of sin. John 3:17 says, "For God sent not his Son into the world to condemn the world; but that the world through him might be saved." Not much is known about Jesus' childhood, but that which may be known of His life and works are recorded throughout the New Testament writings, specifically in the gospel writings of Matthew, Mark, Luke, and John. As the result of the early Jews rejecting his coming as King of the Jews or as the Messiah, the message of redemption and the forgiveness of sins through Jesus Christ was preached to the Gentiles, who would be saved by Him through faith, as written throughout the writings of the apostle Paul.

Though Jesus came in the flesh as the Son of God, He is the image of His Father. When the disciple Philip requested that Jesus show all the disciples the Father and said that would prove His deity, Jesus responded by saying, ". . . Have I been so long time with you, and yet hast thou not known me, Philip? He that hath seen me hath seen the Father; and how sayest thou then, Shew us the Father?" (John 14:9). There is only one true God, ubiquitous and eternal, the creator of the heavens and the earth, who is above all things. Jesus bore the image of God the Father on earth. Paul, in his first letter to Timothy, said it this way, "For there is one God, and one mediator between God and men, the man Christ Jesus;" (1 Timothy 2:5). It is clearly obvious that the name of Jesus is not just an ordinary household name to be used in every imaginable context, but it is to be revered and honored as holy.

During the life of Jesus on earth, He did many mighty and miraculous signs and wonders, none of which had ever been seen by humankind. John

21:25 states, "And there are also many other things which Jesus did, the which, if they should be written every one, I suppose that even the world itself could not contain the books that should be written. Amen."

During His earthly ministry, Jesus preached the resurrection of the dead of which He was the first fruit. He declared how He must go to Jerusalem and suffer many things from the elders, chief priests, and scribes of that day, and that after being killed, he would rise again on the third day (Matthew 16:21). After his crucifixion, his resurrection from the dead by the Spirit of God was first witnessed by Mary Magdalene, Joanna, Mary the mother of James, and other women who went to the grave with sweet spices that they might anoint his body, only to find an empty tomb (Luke 24:1-3). After hearing the report from these women who were the first humans to visit the sepulcher, Jesus appeared to the woman of whom He cast out seven devils, Mary Magdalene (Mark 16:9). Afterwards, He showed Himself alive to two other disciples as they were walking (Mark 16:12). Eventually Jesus appeared to all of the chosen remaining disciples, and gave them what is considered by many theologians as the Great Commission, saying, ". . . Go ye into all the world, and preach the gospel to every creature (Mark 16:15).

Before His ascension to heaven, Jesus gave his apostles whom He had chosen instructions to wait in the city of Jerusalem until they received the promise of the Father: power from on high, the Holy Ghost. It is also recorded in the first chapter of the book of Acts how the apostles gazed up toward heaven as Jesus was taken up into a cloud out of their sight. This must have been a remarkable encounter for them to behold. As they watched with amazement, two angels who stood nearby comforted them by saying, ". . . this same Jesus, which is taken up from you into heaven, shall so come in like manner as ye have seen him go into heaven" (Acts 1:9-11). Hallelujah, praise God!

The apostle Paul also writes:

For the Lord himself shall descend from heaven with a shout, with the voice of the archangel, and with the trump of God: and the dead in Christ shall rise first: Then we which are alive and remain shall be caught up together with them in the clouds, to meet the Lord in the air: and so shall we ever be with the Lord (1 Thessalonians 4:16-17).

It is also important to realize that God as Father is one with the Son and the Holy Ghost. There are not three separate Gods. Many Bible interpreters and scholars would argue differently on this issue. For greater clarity, 1 John 5:7 states, "For there are three that bear record in heaven, the Father, the Word, and the Holy Ghost: and these three are one." For example, it is possible for me to be a father, a son, an uncle, a business owner, and a pastor, while yet being the same person. However, a notable difference between me and God is that I am corporeal, meaning I have a physical body, material and tangible. God however, is a Spirit with the ability to transcend material boundaries that we are not able to transcend right now, though one day every born-again believer's body will be changed from mortal to immortal to be like Jesus. We can only be in one place at any given time, but God can be everywhere, all of the time, and still be undiminished as God.

This chapter of who Jesus is cannot provide a complete or detailed insight of His existence or His workings. I suggest doing a thorough study of the gospels to get a broader awareness about the life of Jesus. However, to truly know Him spiritually, a person must be born-again and baptized with the Holy Ghost, who reveals the Godhead. In one of the apostle Paul's letters to the church at Corinth, he wrote: "Wherefore I give you to understand, that no man speaking by the Spirit of God calleth Jesus accursed: and that no man can say that Jesus is Lord, but by the Holy Ghost" (1 Corinthians 12:3).

His purpose on earth has long been believed to unify, but the truth is that He was polarizing. Jesus said, "Suppose ye that I am come to give peace on earth? I tell you, Nay; but rather division" (Luke 12:51). Certainly, He came to reconcile mankind back to God through His atoning death, and as mankind resumes his relationship with the Father through spiritual rebirth, mankind should become separated from the behaviors of the ungodly.

Therefore, I encourage believers and unbelievers to seek the Lord Jesus Christ, hope in the grace given to us by Him for eternal salvation, and escape the judgment that is to come upon earth according to this saying by Jesus: "Watch ye therefore, and pray always, that ye may be accounted worthy to escape all these things that shall come to pass, and to stand before the Son of man" (Luke 21:36).

CHAPTER TWO
What's in a Name?

One mistake may not permanently define you as an individual,
but it can mar your name or reputation for a long time.

Names carry a greater significance than typically thought about. Everything in life is associated with some type of name recognition. Greatness and shame are two distinct recognition categories. Great athletes, nations, cities, leaders, and businesses each have names that make them very recognizable, and with that comes significant features, accomplishments, and/or historical references, associated with their names, that makes them highly notable. There are professional sports teams which have championship grandeur (e.g., the Boston Celtics, Los Angeles Lakers, New England Patriots, Green Bay Packers, Edmonton Oilers and others), and their names certainly distinguish them from other teams with lessor distinction or fame. Most people have heard about these teams, and many athletes feel honored to play on such storied franchises. However, there have been professional athletes, it didn't matter what team they played on, whose names brought great recognition and attention, e.g., Michael Jordan, who is best known for his thirteen playing years with the Chicago Bulls. Toward the end of his basketball-playing career, he played two years with the Washington Wizards. The Washington Wizards became more recognizable after Michael joined the team, because most people were following him as a player, hoping his teams were either successful or unsuccessful. There have also been great political figures who are more renowned than other similar figures. There are nations whose names are associated with greatness or lesser power. From these examples, we understand that there is something in a name, whether good or bad.

Nothing or no one who has ever been considered great, notable, celebrated, famed, or distinguished takes delight in a lesser consideration. Even God delights in praise of Himself. Exodus 34:14 states, "For thou shalt worship no other god: for the LORD, whose name is Jealous, is a jealous God." Psalm 47:7 also states, "For God is the King of all the earth: sing ye praises with understanding." Therefore, it is clear and obvious throughout Scripture that God does not take pleasure or delight in any disdain of His name or character, nor any other repugnant and adverse characterizations or actions against Himself, who is Holy.

Proverbs 22:1 says: "A good name is rather to be chosen than great riches, and loving favour rather than silver and gold." I think it is safe to say that most people care about their name and having a good reputation in the community and among associations. Most people would appreciate not being known under criminal, scandalous, crooked, or corrupt name titles, e.g., rapist, or titles and headings which carry shame. Once a name is negatively labelled, it becomes difficult to sway or change the opinions of others otherwise. Some people simply prefer to talk about the negative aspects of people, because that makes for good barber shop talk.

Every now and then, I would receive a warning notice in the mail of someone in the surrounding area whose picture was plastered on a card noting they were registered as a sex offender. These notices are sent to make the public aware of those who are guilty of having sex with a minor, child pornography, rapists, and other forms of sexual assault. Their names, aliases, addresses, and other relevant information is made known to the community in which they live. It would seem that these individuals are marred for the rest of their lives. I think most of us would rather have a good name than have all the money in the world. Money cannot buy a good name when someone is always doing bad things. Having integrity may not be widely acceptable or popular, but it is better to have it than not.

There are also situations where people desire to protect the integrity of family names. When a family business name has become a name of dishonor, it is normally because of some negative behavior by one or more of the members of the family, and others may stereotype everyone in the family business because of one family member. In some situations, the person whose name brings shame upon a family business is usually removed from public communication or contact to minimize further scrutiny and shame to the business. Using fictitious business names are usually preferred over family-named businesses for this reason.

Institutional name types, e.g., for churches, governments, law enforcement, etc., also are marred by negativity because of the lack of integrity by one or many of its participants or members and may never be seen or appreciated for what they were truly meant to represent. Lately, we have seen prominent and professional figures in entertainment, theater, business, and politics have their names recognized for all of the wrong reasons. In addition, there have been religious leaders, particularly those who are of the Christian faith, who have conducted themselves in a manner inconsistent with the traditions, values, and teachings of Christ. These actions not only bring discredit upon the individual, but they also bring disgrace upon the Christian faith and upon the church as an institution, just as they do on other recognizable organizations where violations of integrity occur. Therefore, we can understand just how significant it is to have recognizable *name integrity*, and how much more so than with the name of Jesus Christ.

God is concerned about believers maintaining a sense of pride and integrity in His name as His children. Though Jesus was falsely accused by the Jews, chief priests, scribes, and elders of His day, those accusations were part of the process of Him being sent to die for our sins. This should be a reminder that we are to expect similar persecution for identifying with Christ, while not forsaking the dignity of suffering as children of God. Certainly, every true believer will be reproached for the name of Christ, but Scripture also cautions us against suffering as murderers, thieves, evildoers, and busybodies in other people's matters and states that if we suffer as Christians, we should glorify God (1 Peter 4:15-16).

Jesus Christ is the righteousness of God. When the disciples of Jesus asked Him to teach them how to pray, Jesus replied, "... When ye pray, say, Our Father which art in heaven, Hallowed be thy name ..." (Luke 11:2). To hallow a name is to consider it holy, sacred; to consecrate and sanctify it. The Old Testament mentions several names of God, but in this writing, I am going to focus on the New Testament name of Jesus.

The apostle Paul wrote in his letter to the church at Philippi that the name Jesus, when referring to the Son of God, is the most prestigious and honorable name ever bestowed on anyone and that God had highly exalted Jesus, and had given Him a name which is above every name. He further states that every knee should bow to Him—whether of things in heaven, in earth, and things under the earth—and every mouth should confess that Jesus is the Lord to the glory of God the Father (Philippians 2:9-11). His name is holy and reverend, meaning he is to be feared, revered, honored, and worshipped. I would never want anyone to consider me as reverend because I believe that is a designation reserved only for God, and mankind having sin, is not worthy of this distinguished name recognition. This is a persuasion or conviction that I sincerely hold, but there are many members of clergy who have no disapproval of being called reverend, which is understood based on denominational constructs. I don't believe mankind should be classified under headings descriptive of Almighty God, but rather should live holy lives. Psalm 111:9 says, "He sent redemption unto his people: he hath commanded his covenant forever: holy and reverend is his name." Reverend in the Hebrew means to fear, so in this context, God's name is fearful, dreadful, and terrible, and therefore inspires reverence, godly fear, and awe. Other than the name of Jesus, names given to humans at birth does not equate to any degree of reverence or divinity, regardless of what has been accomplished or achieved in life. Jesus said in Matthew 23:8-9 when talking to the multitude and to His disciples, "But be not ye called Rabbi: for one is your Master, even Christ; and all ye are brethren. And call no man your father upon the earth: for one is your Father, which is in heaven." Some may think this is far-fetched, and others as nonsensical, but these are the words of Christ. Those who walk in humility before God does not seek this recognition of honor and reverence upon themselves.

It is through the name of Jesus that demons tremble and are cast out. It is through the name of Jesus that many people were miraculous healed and freed from various forms of spiritual bondage. It was through the name of Jesus that the early disciples and apostles were empowered to carry forth the mandate given to them by Christ Jesus. His name is the only name given to us whereby we are saved. When Peter and John went to the temple for prayer, they encountered a man lame from birth who every day would be laid at the entry gate of the temple to ask for a donation. Amazingly, Peter and John had a different response to the lame man than others, and they told him that they didn't have any money, but that which they did have, they would freely give to him. They said to the man, ". . . In the name of Jesus Christ of Nazareth rise up and walk" (Acts 3:6). Then they took him by the right hand and pulled him to his feet, and he was miraculously healed. Because the crowd was greatly bewildered, Peter began to preach Jesus as the explanation for this mighty act, saying to the crowd, "And his name through faith in his name hath made this man strong, whom ye see and know . . ." (Acts 3:16). What an awesome God we serve!

Jesus' power is still relevant today in our lives. We pray to the Father in His name. We call upon His name when we're in trouble. There are many miracles, signs and wonders associated with His name. In Mark's gospel, Jesus is on record saying:

> And these signs shall follow them that believe; In my name shall they cast out devils; they shall speak with new tongues; They shall take up serpents; and if they drink any deadly thing, it shall not hurt them; they shall lay hands on the sick, and they shall recover (Mark 16:17-18).

The apostle Paul writes, "And whatsoever ye do in word or deed, do all in the name of the Lord Jesus, giving thanks to God and the Father by him" (Colossians 3:17). Far too often, today's ministers have spoken haughtily by using words such as *I*, *me*, or *my* when describing things done as opposed to giving the credit to God. Godly fear and humility should be factored into the actions and responses of every believer in keeping with the traditions of giving God the glory, as did the earlier church. Many Christians tend to be self-centered who seek attention through their gifts. I call this *glory chasing*. When a church or individual is excelling in the things of God, care should be taken not to substitute the name of Jesus as the source of all miracles and mighty acts. Acts 14 mentions an experience that the apostles Paul and Barnabas had as they preached in the city of Lystra when a man cripple from birth was healed. When the people saw what was done, they shouted, ". . . The gods are come down to us in the likeness of men" (Acts 14:11). The priest of the pagan god Jupiter began to offer a sacrifice to honor Paul and Barnabas as gods, but the apostles quickly halted the priest, saying, ". . . Sirs, why do ye these things? We also are men of like passions with you, and preach unto you that ye should turn from these vanities unto the living God, which made heaven, and earth, and the sea, and all things that are therein" (Acts 14:15). God also spoke through the prophet Isaiah saying, "I am the Lord: that is my name: and my glory will I not give to another, neither my praise to graven images" (Isaiah 42:8).

How would you desire Jesus to be known or remembered? I encourage every believer to be diligent in establishing and guarding Jesus' name integrity.

CHAPTER THREE

The Church of Jesus Christ

*"And now I am no more in the world, but these are in the world,
and I come to thee. Holy Father, keep through thine own name
those whom thou hast given me, that they may be one, as we are"*
(John 17:11).

The word *church* has taken on so many definitions in modern society. Ephesians 4:4-6 states in a letter penned by the apostle Paul to the Christians at Ephesus while imprisoned at Rome:

There is one body, and one Spirit, even as ye are called in one hope of your calling; One Lord, one faith, one baptism, One God and Father of all, who is above all, and through all, and in you all.

The reputation and status of the church of God in Christ in this present time has been vastly affected because of how it is being represented and perceived by believers and nonbelievers. It must be first considered that there would not be any mention of a Christian church had it not been for what the Lord Jesus Christ said to Simon Peter in Matthew 16:18: "And I say also unto thee, that thou art Peter, and upon this rock I will build my church; and the gates of hell shall not prevail against it." Upon saying this, Jesus was establishing His ministry on earth among mankind through Peter's revelation that Jesus was the Christ, the Son of the living God, and that the church should bear the image, glory, and power of His name through the Spirit perpetually throughout all generations.

Traditionally, the word church has so many different meanings to so many different people, not all of which are compatible with a true and holy God. To some people, the church is simply a building. To others, it may be a gathering of people, unified for the common purpose of worship to a god or goddess, but not necessarily the Father of the Lord Jesus Christ. I feel safe in saying that for the majority of people, it is a place to go to keep pace with traditional norms of church, to ease the guilt associated with a sin, and to seek entertainment, motivation, and spiritual uplifting. The perceptions of church will vary from culture to culture, experience to experience, and belief to belief; but one thing is sure, the church where Jesus Christ is Lord and Savior is the only representation of His body on earth. Contrary to the church of Jesus Christ is the church of Satan, which opposes everything Christ died for; even having its own Bible.

There are several words used to refer to a church, such as, abbey, basilica, mosque, shrine, synagogue, or temple, which typically are building structures. However, in every instance, a church is a legitimate word with a legitimate purpose, but let's dig deeper into its true meaning and purpose as intended by God.

The church of Jesus Christ is more than an institution with government; it is an institution of righteousness through faith in Jesus Christ. The Greek word for church is *ekklēsia*, and it is defined as a calling out, especially of a religious congregation of members on earth or saints in heaven or both; an assembly. In the Christian context, it is an assembly of born-again believers united together to carry out God's plans on earth, and whose hope for eternal salvation is through faith in the Lord Jesus Christ. It is important to emphasize that the church is an orderly institution that manages its affairs according to prescribed regulations for the body of Christ in terms of worship and civil governance. The Bible is the governing document for church affairs and is the infallible, trustworthy, and accurate written Word of God to the churches of God in Christ. 2 Timothy 3:16 says, "All Scripture is given by inspiration of God, and is profitable for doctrine, for reproof, for correction, for instruction in righteousness."

When discussing church integrity, the standard will always be according to God, not according to mankind. One of the challenges that the true church of Christ faces is the infiltration of so many different church types across the world. And because of so many gods to worship with religious freedoms in the Unites States of America, the message of Christ has become diluted and muddled in the chaos of people trying to figure out who or what is the true God; what is the correct doctrine, or what is the most accurate interpretation of His message to mankind.

The nuances associated with scriptural and doctrinal applications have caused a divide among believers and churches. It is amazing that bishops, pastors, and denominational leaders cannot come together to resolve doctrinal disputes that affect Christian unity. However, it is no surprise that it is occurring; Scripture has already warned us.

1 Timothy 4:1 states, "Now the Spirit speaketh expressly, that in the latter times some shall depart from the faith, giving heed to seducing spirits, and doctrines of devils." It is apparent that Satan is behind the mass effort to distort the image of the Christian church.

Therefore, God is speaking pointedly and distinctively through chosen men and women of the body of Christ who have heard his voice, have not compromised, and have become burdened with the way of error that is collapsing and destroying the fabric of Christian integrity in homes, churches, governments, schools, and other institutions. There is a clarion call of God upon the heart of the believer to return to a place of dignity and respect in the body of Christ; a call to holiness. The world and the unsaved will be gravely affected if Christians falter in responding to their duty and obligation to uphold and preserve the standards of integrity in the Christian church. It is recorded in Matthew 5:13-16 where Jesus said to His disciples:

> Ye are the salt of the earth: but if the salt has lost his savour, wherewith shall it be salted? it is henceforth good for nothing, but to be cast out, and to be trodden under foot of men. Ye are the light of the world. A city that is set on an hill cannot be hid. Neither do men light a candle, and put it under a bushel, but on a candlestick; and it giveth light unto all that are in the house. Let your light so shine before men, that they may see your good works, and glorify your Father which is in heaven.

Every Christian should partake in the ministry of reconciling people's hearts to the truth of God. Paul emphasizes the responsibility of reconciled believers as new creatures in Christ, being agents of God to the unsaved, sharing with them the gospel of grace that thereby they also, upon believing, may be reconciled to God through the blood of Christ (2 Corinthians 5:18). We are to "make straight paths for [our] feet, lest that which is lame be turned out of the way; but let it rather be healed" (Hebrews 12:13).

The church of Jesus Christ is considered the body of Christ which has many members. The apostle Paul writes in 1 Corinthians 12:12-14:

> For as the body is one, and hath many members, and all the members of that one body, being many, are one body: so also is Christ. For by one Spirit are we all baptized into one body,

whether we be Jews and Gentiles, whether we be bond or free; and have been all made to drink into one Spirit. For the body is not one member, but many.

One of the major problems facing the church in this modern age is the diversity of representations. There are numerous religious denominations, churches, and ministry types formed under the name of Jesus. However, doctrines differ and many believers find it difficult accepting anything outside of their own church doctrine, even denouncing other churches as fraudulent. This is an instance of flawed and broken fellowship among the churches of God, and because of it, *fellowship integrity* is affected.

We must also reach across color and gender markers, making them nonexistent; we must accept our differences in the body of Christ without discarding each other. There "should be no schism in the body [of Christ], but that the members should have the same care one for another" (1 Corinthians 12:25). It is also mentioned in Galatians 5:15, "But if ye bite and devour one another, take heed that ye be not consumed one of another." Beloved, this is not the will of God, neither should it be the character or behavior of the redeemed of the Lord. The church of Jesus Christ is the greatest institution ever formed, and I am proud to be part of it. The church of Jesus Christ looks flawed to many unbelievers, but it is not; the believer's love and faith is yet being perfected. What is flawed is everything outside of Christ, and this was the primary reason for His coming. He is the author and captain of our salvation. As high priest, He lives forever, and His kingdom is everlasting. God's plan is to unify all believers together with Christ as head.

In early 2005, God gave me instructions to write the following article, "A Repenting Church," not as a pastor, but as someone moved by the Holy Spirit and carrying the burden of the Lord. It remains relevant today.

A Repenting Church

We're in the closing days of the church. God has released the latch, the door is in motion, and we don't know the distance the door has to travel before it completely closes.

This is the deception that has crept into the church that is in the minds of many people: that the visible church is actually the true church of God. Pastors and leaders of God's people are responsible for diffusing this deception. To understand this deception, let's look closer at the visible church. It is often understood to be simply an organization. However, the true church of God is an organization and a living organism; it has a body. What many of us see are churches with diverse appearances, conflicting purposes, and divisions between each other. The true focus and purpose of the church has been diminished. It has become a side show and a place for religious entertainment where many believers wear imaginary costumes as though masquerading to be approved by God and others. When the session or service has ended, and the benediction given, there remains a lifestyle of carnality and ungodly behavior until the next scheduled service where the acts are repeated. This has become an alarming, yet popular trend in churches. Entertainment is often used to supplant genuine worship. John 4:24 says, "God is a Spirit: and they that worship him must worship him in spirit and in truth."

For the most part, people gather in different religious orders, attend to rituals of prayer, singing, and preaching, but rarely is there a noticeable change in character that reflects the character of God. Sinners and those who don't know Christ must see Him through the blood-washed and redeemed, those whose sins have been forgiven and who are living Christ-centered lifestyles. 2 Corinthians 5:17 says, "Therefore if any man be in Christ, he is a new creature: old things are passed away; behold, all things are become new."

Sermons are preached from pulpits. Choirs, praise singers and praise dancers perform, but a lot of Christians fail to demonstrate the fruit of a Spirit-filled life. Congregations are encouraged in the things of God; missionaries and ambassadors are sent to foreign countries to provide food, clothing, medicines, and to minister the Gospel of Christ; and we organize conventions for empowerment, spiritual enrichment, and even functions for pleasure and social enjoyment. While all of these things are good, they're often overshadowed with incidents of misbehavior by members of the clergy and lay members, and therefore the church's presence on the earth is diminished or weakened by negative stereotypes. Matthew 5:13 says that Christians are the salt of the earth, but if the salt has lost its ability to flavor, represent, and witness Christ, how else can it be used? It is therefore good for nothing, but to be thrown out and trodden under the foot of men.

God is not pleased with the manner in which we live. Regarding the church at Ephesus, Revelation 2:4 states, "Nevertheless I have somewhat against thee, because thou hast left thy first love." It would be hard to convince many today that they may have left their first love for God, because they feel justified by false standards, but this Scripture also has relevance to the modern-era church. Many would argue that everything is fine and disagree with this spiritual assessment because of spiritual blindness, closing their eyes, ears, and heart to the truth of God's message to the church.

Revelation 2:5 says, "Remember therefore from whence thou art fallen, and repent, and do the first works; or else I will come unto thee quickly, and will remove thy candlestick out of his place, except thou repent." ~End

There was a time, and many will agree, when there was a heartfelt passion and craving for the things of the Kingdom of God. Believers would seek God in earnest prayer and fasting; many would spend hours studying the Bible, grasping for all that heaven has to offer. When times were lean, the people of God as well as families were closer to each other. Prayer was prevalent in our schools and there was more reverence for God. But as we've moved from that state of mind, conditions have worsened. Proverbs 14:34 says, "Righteousness exalteth a nation: but sin is a reproach to any people." Satan (the devil) has become bolder in his efforts to destroy the minds of our youth and adults; there is little shame for some of the most lewdness of acts. The family structure has become shattered and redefined, while violence and crime are on the rise.

In addition, many believers find themselves searching for the truest fellowship of Christian believers in our churches. While we understand that there is not a perfect physical Church, there must still be the influential power of God through the Holy Spirit operating in and through the lives of his people. Without this demonstration of power, Satan is granted greater access to infiltrate and control. The Spirit of falsehood and hypocrisy has already taken position within Church ranks. Pastors and leaders are not as effective in leading God's people into wholesome relationships with God because Satan is deceiving them. This can be partly attributed to disobedience to God and worldly desires. The truth of God is also being diluted and interpreted in such a manner that it minimizes the requirement to live in reverence to God.

I've spoken to believers who feel left out, as though they have no self-worth unless they have a certain financial standing or some other acceptable status. Jesus came for every person's benefit. The Church, in the opinion of some, has become an environment of prejudice, and materialistic obsession and possession, and this is partly true. Jeremiah 2:4-5, 8 states:

Hear ye the word of the Lord, O house of Jacob, and all the families of the house of Israel: Thus saith the Lord, What iniquity have your fathers found in me, that they are gone far from me, and have walked after vanity, and are become vain? ... The priests said not, Where is the Lord? and they that handle the law knew me not: the pastors also transgressed against me, and the prophets prophesied by Baal, and walked after things that do not profit.

There is an increase of Satan's influence within the physical church and in the world, which is a sign of the end of the age.

God has instructed me to warn his people concerning the Scripture found in Jeremiah 2, most significantly verses 11-13. This nation, even its Christian citizens, has exchanged the glory of God upon their lives for that which does not profit. God is also saying that His people, those who have been called and chosen of God, have committed two evils: they have forsaken Him, the fountain of living waters, and have cut out, hewed, and designed for themselves faulty or cracked cisterns that cannot hold water. In Mark 8:36 Jesus said, "For what shall it profit a man, if he shall gain the whole world, and lose his own soul?" God also says in 2 Chronicles 7:14, "If my people, which are called by my name, shall humble themselves, and pray, and seek my face, and turn from their wicked ways; then will I hear from heaven, and will forgive their sin, and will heal their land." Anything outside of this will be unacceptable. Wake up, people of God!

2 Timothy 3:1-5 says:

This know also, that in the last days perilous times shall come. For men shall be lovers of their own selves, covetous, boasters, proud, blasphemers, disobedient to parents, unthankful, unholy, without natural affection, trucebreakers, false accusers, incontinent, fierce, despisers of those that are good, traitors, heady, high-minded, lovers of pleasures more than lovers of God; Having a form of godliness, but denying the power thereof: from such turn away.

Only through God can we take back the things that Satan, the devil, has taken from us. The church of God must become more aggressive against evil and less divisive against each other. 2 Corinthians 10:4 says, "For the weapons of our warfare are not carnal, but mighty through God to the pulling down of strongholds." Ephesians 6:12 says, "For we wrestle not against flesh and blood, but against principalities, against powers, against the rulers of the darkness of this world, against spiritual wickedness in high places." I salute all of my fellow laborers in the cause of Jesus Christ. Be strong and of good might. ~

Probably one of the most difficult things about being a messenger of the Lord who is given instructions to speak is that the messenger usually appears to be sitting in a seat of judgment. The fact is that God has always chosen vessels to warn and speak on His behalf for a multiplicity of reasons.

"Jesus Christ the same yesterday, and to day, and for ever" (Hebrews 13:8).

CHAPTER FOUR

What is integrity?

*"The integrity of the upright shall guide them: but the perverseness
of transgressors shall destroy them"
(Proverbs 11:3).*

So far, I have not given a specific definition for integrity, but through-out this chapter and subsequent chapters, I will be discussing several applications of integrity. *Integrity is not defined as human faultlessness, in any sense of the word.* However, integrity can be summarized as adherence to certain principles that governs character and judgment. It is to be undiminished from operating with proper codes of personal conduct. It is the unimpaired existence of a person's ability to differentiate between right and wrong.

Integrity in biblical applications means uprightness, completeness, and innocence, but it is not a word or expression restricted to a Christian culture, nor is it restricted to any one group, organization, or industry. It is a behavioral trait that is beneficial, when applied, to all who embrace it as the fundamental way of living and doing business. Unfortunately, portions of our society are not governed by integrity, but there are many organizations, businesses, churches, and individuals that place integrity at the core of its principles for conducting affairs.

Many people will acknowledge that integrity may be the right way, but not the only way. The majority of decisions, methods, manners, and life choices are driven by some conscientious perspective of what is right or wrong, true or false, good or bad, and in many circumstances, success and failure, but imagine that in each of these scenarios, integrity is integrated into the process. What would businesses, churches, governments, schools, marriage, and other personal relationships and involvements be like if each were governed by integrity? You may be thinking that's too good of a world, and certainly unattainable; I agree. However, while that may be true, it is still something to be emphasized at every level of our existence. Sin makes it impossible to have a perfect world, but that does not prevent mankind from having integrity. When speaking of integrity, many people would probably say, "No one is perfect." But this phrase demonstrates a misunderstanding of integrity.

The right way of doing things is usually determined from a set of prescribed rules, standards, traditions, procedures, and protocols, and we respect them. However, there could be distinct and necessary variations from a prescribed way to achieve a desired outcome, and these variations are usually instinctive and at times spontaneous responses to unforeseen situations. For instance, your job has a procedure to follow in a normal situation, but to follow that procedure does not appear to be the right thing to do because of an unusual occurrence, so you modify or disobey that procedure for all of the right reasons; possibly to save a life or avoid some other tragic outcome. The question then becomes, "What is influencing or guiding your actions?" We can clearly see that regardless of prescribed methods, standards, or procedures, each individual has the power and ability to be guided by his or her own sense of integrity, which may be later questioned. There may be situations when doing something may be considered wrong, but doing it as the best choice and with good intentions could also be considered an act of integrity, especially when the outcome is favorable in all aspects. Proverbs 16:2 reminds us that all of our ways, customs, and traditions may be right in our own eyes, but God measures the intent of our spirit; He ponders the motives of our heart when responding to us.

Looking at actions through this lens may lead to much speculation and misunderstanding, particularly for those who are blind to certain principles and who only see life as black or white. With everything made, written, or prescribed by people, there will be imperfections which may require corrections in order to achieve desirable outcomes. From the example above we can conclude that, from a *natural perspective*, integrity does not always follow a prescribed procedure or way, but the prescribed procedure or way should be designed and written with desirable outcomes as the ultimate goal. This is also considered integrity.

From the Kingdom of God's perspective, integrity is the prescribed way, the right way, and the only way, without controversy or alteration. It operates under one government and school of thought: God's. Psalms 19:7-11 says:

> The law of the LORD is perfect, converting the soul: the testimony of the LORD is sure, making wise the simple. The statutes of the LORD are right, rejoicing the heart: the commandment of the LORD is pure, enlightening the eyes. The fear of the LORD is clean, enduring forever: the judgments of the LORD are true and righteous altogether. More to be desired are they than gold, yea, than much fine gold: sweeter also than honey and the honeycomb. Moreover, by them is thy servant warned: and in keeping of them there is great reward.

For every true believer in Christ, possessing integrity should not be an option. It houses good values, good intentions, and good works. Integrity is God's preferred way, and it is paralleled with living holy. There are no exceptions for the believer in Christ but to live holy lives. The apostle Peter says in 1 Peter 1:15-16, "But as he which hath called you is holy, so be ye holy in all manner of conversation; Because it is written, Be ye holy; for I am holy." Peter was speaking about this requirement of the Father, and for some reason in many of today's churches, the word *holy* is rarely heard, and many confessing believers appear upset when it is presented to them.

As aforementioned, many people will challenge the message of integrity on the premise that no one is perfect, and they usually rely on these Scriptures to support their position:

+ John 8:7, "…He that is without sin among you, let him first cast a stone at her." Jesus said this to the finger pointers of a woman taken in adultery.
+ 1 John 1:8, "If we say that we have no sin, we deceive ourselves, and the truth is not in us."
+ Romans 3:23, "For all have sinned, and come short of the glory of God."

Integrity is a place where the honor of God dwells.

Each of these Scriptures acknowledges the condition of sin that came upon all flesh after Adam disobeyed God in the Garden of Eden. I am not attempting to convince anyone of sinless perfection. However, those who rely on and quote only the above Scriptures have limited understanding of the will of God. Throughout Scripture, God speaks against sin; therefore, as saints, we cannot condone sinful lifestyles and lustful appetites as acceptable, though we have sin. Jesus came to forgive us of all sin through

His atoning blood. 1 John 1:9 says, "If we confess our sins, he is faithful and just to forgive us our sins, and to cleanse us from all unrighteousness."

Is it Okay?

Integrity will always ask, "Is it okay to do something in question?" Integrity means not taking the grace of God in vain or using it improperly. The current acceptable belief and doctrine in many churches and among many believers today is that "God will forgive you, so it's okay to do it." This seems to be a new definition of grace being taught and applied, and it is meant to eliminate feeling convicted for wrongdoings or living contrary to sound doctrine. It draws its support from Romans 5:20 where it states, "Moreover the law entered, that the offence might abound. But where sin abounded, grace did much more abound."

I am not giving a complete analysis of grace in this chapter, but I will discuss it in more detail in a later chapter. However, I will say that grace should be understood to be more than just God's unmerited favor. It is the means by which God administers salvation, strength, and every good thing upon everyone through Jesus Christ. It is not administered for purposes of fleshly gratification through sin. Romans 6:1-2 states, "What shall we say then? Shall we continue in sin, that grace may abound? God forbid. How shall we, that are dead to sin, live any longer therein? Further in the chapter it says the believers should consider themselves to be dead to sin, but alive unto God through Jesus Christ our Lord (Romans 6:11).

To further understand the liberty given through grace, we must also understand our freedom from the Old Testament law given through Moses. God initially gave laws to man to govern him. Genesis 6:5 says, "And GOD saw that the wickedness of man was great in the earth, and that every imagination of the thoughts of his heart was only evil continually." From this we can see how important it was to govern man in some acceptable manner. We're all familiar with the great flood God sent upon earth that killed everything except Noah, his family, and the animals that were brought onto the ark (Genesis 7:23). God realized afterwards that sin had not been eradicated and vowed not to destroy the earth again with flooding (Genesis 9:11).

Subsequently in Genesis 17, we see God calling Abraham and his seed to be His people, who he would later bring out of four hundred years of Egyptian captivity through Moses, giving them laws and commandments to govern them. Seeing that His people kept disobeying His laws, commandments, and statutes, He sent them into Babylonian captivity for seventy years until they returned through expeditions led by Zerubbabel, Ezra, and Nehemiah to restore worship, rebuilding the temple, and the walls around Jerusalem. The point I'm attempting to make with this short narrative of Jewish history is that it's not okay to do wrong. It wasn't okay then, and it's not okay now. God spoke through Jeremiah the Prophet in Jeremiah 31:33, saying, "...But this shall be the covenant that I will make with the house of Israel; After those days, saith the LORD, I will put my law in their inward parts, and write it in their hearts; and will be their God, and they shall be my people."

Jesus Christ came as the ultimate answer to the condition of sin, and after His resurrection and ascension, He would send the Holy Spirit to live in the heart of His children as promised. The Holy Spirit would "reprove the world of sin, of righteousness, and of judgment" (John 16:7-8). The Holy Ghost is the power and governor of God in the heart, and He draws the believer into deeper intimacy with Him. The born-again believer who is Holy Ghost filled does not accept sin as an acceptable thing to practice.

Paul says in Romans 10:4, "For Christ is the end of the law for righteousness to every one that believeth." He also states in Romans 6:14-15, "For sin shall not have dominion over you: for ye are not under the law, but under grace. What then? Shall we sin, because we are not under the law, but under grace? God forbid." He writes in his letter to Timothy that the law is good if a man uses it lawfully. He then adds, "Knowing this, that the law is not made for a righteous man

. . . (1 Timothy 1:8-10). I strongly suggest reading verses 9-10 for a detailed list of who the law was made for. This does not mean Christians are exempt from the law. It is written in the law given to Moses that one shalt not kill. Does that mean we can kill now because the law is done away with? No. The righteousness of the law was fulfilled in Christ for us, and the Holy Spirit sent by God to the believer convicts mankind when he is in violation of God's righteousness, but without a death sentence, because he is now under grace. God chastens those He love, and afflicts every son (Hebrews 12:6). Romans 8:1-9 speaks a lot about the law of the Spirit of life in Christ Jesus which frees us from the law of sin and death. The Spirit-filled believer is the believer with the Spirit of Christ dwelling inside, who obeys the will of God in their lives. Ephesians 5:18 admonishes the church by saying, "And be not drunk with wine, wherein is excess; but be filled with the Spirit." One of the most interesting scriptures for many believers to understand or accept is found in Romans 8:9 where it says, ". . . Now if any man have not the Spirit of Christ, he is none of his." There are many people who teach that the Spirit of Christ is in every believer. However, evidence of His abiding presence is witnessed through a believer's life of holiness, love, devotion, and obedience to the things of God.

God does not have separate spirits for Baptists, Catholics, Methodists, Pentecostals, or any other unique denominational group. 1 Corinthians 12:13 says, "For by one Spirit are we all baptized into one body, whether we be Jews or Gentiles, whether we be bond or free; and have been all made to drink into one Spirit." The evidence of Christ in a person is also witnessed through their passionate desires to please Him, not from going to church only, as so many believe. Philippians 2:13 gives greater clarity by saying, "For it is God which worketh in you both to will and to do of his good pleasure." We therefore conclude, it is not okay to live in disregard of God's grace for the purpose of practicing sin and living ungodly as confessing believers. It is truly a full-time life of living with Jesus' name integrity.

1 John 2:29 says, "If ye know that he is righteous, ye know that every one that doeth righteousness is born of him." 1 John 3:7 gives further credence by saying, "Little children, let no man deceive you: he that doeth righteousness is righteous, even as he is righteous." Integrity speaks on this wise: "We fall, but we get up. We sin, and we ask forgiveness." The believer should not grow weary endeavoring to do things the right way, especially in a world filled with corruption, deceit, falsehood, and ungodliness. If anything, we give witness of God's power in grace.

It appears that, in the modern era of religious order and behavior; the next religious trend; the next spiritual movement, and that which is considered to be God's voice; is determined by the most popular things said or done by the most recognized and esteemed personalities. This is also deception.

CHAPTER FIVE

Measuring Integrity

Measuring integrity starts with individual conscience. Measuring integrity may seem like an odd phrase, but measuring is something we do in many life applications; e.g., we measure gas volumes in our vehicles, we measure distances traveled, we measure liquid volumes when cooking, we measure our words in heated exchanges, etc. Basically, measuring is any standard of comparison, estimation, or judgment. How far will a person go in a wrong direction before integrity becomes a factor? When integrity is not measured and factored into life, we may be apprehended for wrongdoing and punished. I would suppose that the average prisoner is incarcerated because of neglecting to deploy integrity into a situation or process, because most applications of integrity involve some degree of human restraint. How far will a person be willing to stray from a path before realizing that their actions will have a certain consequence? The apostle Paul writes in Galatians 6:7, "Be not deceived; God is not mocked: for whatsoever a man soweth, that shall he also reap." Paul also writes in 2 Corinthians 13:5, "Examine yourselves, whether ye be in the faith; prove your own selves. …" The examination and awakening of individual conscience is an important process in measuring integrity.

Conscience Integrity

*Everything pleasing to God in life begins and
ends with conscience integrity, and from
there, every good work is performed.*

It is vitally significant for everyone to have *conscience integrity*. Conscience is the inner sense of what is right or wrong in one's conduct or motives, impelling one toward right action. Every human being has a conscience, even the vilest of persons. If you've ever paid close attention to an infant growing into a toddler and then early childhood, you'll notice at some point that they'll begin to demonstrate signs of a moral conscience. It is not a taught response; rather, it is innate by virtue of being human. After a child does something that he or she believes is wrong, he or she may lie if questioned, or they may seek to conceal the wrongdoing, as many adults would probably do. When someone is tempted to do something immoral or illegal, the conscience weighs in and plays a huge part in the human response.

Our society has many people whose consciences are seared, and they have little or no integrity. Everyone has had areas of failed integrity. All of this is caused by sin. When Adam and Eve ate the fruit of the forbidden tree, their eyes were opened and the impact of their wrong arose in their conscience, so they sewed fig leaves together, making aprons for themselves (Genesis 3:7). This was the beginning of the knowledge of good and evil existing in man's conscience, and it has been this way ever since.

There is not a better way of improving conscience integrity than through the wisdom and teachings of Jesus Christ. Every person has some consciousness of God within, the consciousness of right and wrong, but the deceitfulness and hardness of sin makes the things of God seem of little significance. Romans 1:21 says, "Because that, when they knew God, they glorified him not as God, neither were thankful; but became vain in their imaginations, and their foolish heart was darkened." It further explains in verses 24-25 that God also gave them up to do the things their lust craved after—meaning, whatever they could imagine, they did— and that's how they'll be judged. I strongly encourage every reader to read the entire first chapter of Romans to get a clearer understanding of how God reacts to sin when people give no regard for its consequences.

Ignoring God in the conscience is
as decapacitating the soul.

Restoring Christian conscience integrity also entails having the mind of Christ. Philippians 2:5 states, "Let this mind be in you, which was also in Christ Jesus." It is important to point out that conscience integrity as Christians does not mean we have never had a bad thought or been tempted to do wrong. It doesn't mean we won't do wrong. However, having conscience integrity introduces thoughtful and right governance into our thoughts to dominate our judgments. Because of this, if we do fall or come short of the glory of God, we ask for forgiveness and strength to refrain from immoral and destructive behaviors. Always know that the sinful nature of man, called the flesh, has a self-condemning feature, but God has grace for every misstep we make in life that keeps us in right fellowship with the Father as we daily acknowledge our need for Him and express our love. Psalm 37:23-24 clearly expresses God's love and care for us: "The steps of a good man are ordered by the Lord: and he delighteth in his way. Though he fall, he shall not be utterly cast down: for the Lord upholdeth him with his hand." As I've explained, integrity does not mean a faultless or error-free state in mankind. Humans make mistakes for various reasons, but when responding appropriately according to prescribed moral and spiritual laws, God considers that to be responding with integrity. Proverbs 24:16 states that a just man may fall seven times, but he will keep getting up after each fall. Restoring or establishing conscience integrity is an unending process that requires mental exercise and discipline, and a strict adherence to certain principles and standards of governance.

There is an erroneous grace teaching craze that reduces the conscientiousness of godly integrity. I once heard a daily Christian radio program teaching on grace say that it was ok for a man to commit adultery against his wife because grace covers the transgression. Every day when I travelled as a field technician, I would make myself available to listen to that radio broadcast. The theme of the radio ministry was consistent with their beliefs. Certainly, God has grace to forgive sin, but grace does not condone or even give tacit approval to sin. Titus 2:11-12 says, "For the grace of God that bringeth salvation hath appeared to all men, Teaching us that, denying ungodliness and worldly lust, we should live soberly, righteously, and godly, in this present world;" Certainly, I did not agree with this teaching philosophy, and wanted so badly to call in, but there were other listeners who called in with questions concerning this doctrine but were not allowed to challenge the teaching. They were disconnected from the on-air call and accused of being schismatic and unknowledgeable concerning the grace of God.

The apostle Paul says in Acts 24:16, "And herein do I exercise myself, to have always a conscience void of offence toward God, and toward men." When we reflect on what Jesus said concerning the first and second commandments in Mark 12:30-31, which says that we should first love God with all our heart, soul, mind, and strength; and that we should love our neighbor as we love ourselves, we realize that it parallels how Paul expresses conscience integrity. It's difficult to understand how many people who confess to be part of the church of Jesus Christ struggle to embrace integrity as a Christian way of life.

I also believe this level of conscience integrity should be applied to how personal pets are treated. Christians should have a godly conscience concerning the treatment of pets. I've seen some people treat domesticated animals, especially cats, as though they have no place reserved in society, not realizing that God also created animals. For these reasons, we also appreciate the efforts of animal welfare organizations that are concerned with the health, safety and psychological wellness of animals. It's a matter of doing right things.

CHAPTER SIX
Integrity in Crisis

Your purpose in life will not only hold your greatest joy, it will also hold your greatest pain.

Hardships are one of the hardest areas to have integrity for various reasons. Somewhere, someplace, and somehow, each of us will have some form of adversity in life. Hardship does not discriminate based on gender, nationality, religious affiliation, or any other demographic or social status. It is the one thing that seems to test us the most. I feel safe saying that hardship is the most painful place to learn integrity. Troubles and trials will measure integrity's strength and resolve. Since the beginning of time, great men and women have had tremendous crises. For the most part, a person's accomplishments overshadow the pain and agony associated with reaching them. Of course, success, regardless of how a person defines it, is not always achieved through the same means. It is not an exemption from crisis or hardship, and quite frankly, success is often accompanied by hardships. We will realize this in various vicissitudes and life progressions. When reading about Job's experience in Scripture, the loss of his material riches, children, and health causes us to wonder how he survived, but a careful reading and understanding of his crisis from beginning to end is actually very encouraging. Job was the father of seven sons and three daughters. He also possessed seven thousand sheep, three thousand camels, five hundred yoke of oxen, five hundred she-asses, and a great household (Job 1:2-3). He was considered very rich in every sense of the term and was considered the greatest of all men of the East during his time. But things started to go the other way for Job. He lost all his possessions and all his children were killed. In addition to these losses, his body broke out with boils from the bottom of his feet to the crown of his head. He was certainly feeling the weight of his trouble. To make matters even worse, his wife asked him, do you insist on keeping your integrity? You should curse God and die (Job 2:9). Even his personal friends came against him with statements they believed explained his hardship. In Job 14:1 we discover this wisdom, "Man that is born of a woman is of few days, and full of trouble." Even though Job's friends meddled in his affairs, he said to them that, "God forbid that I should justify you: until I die, I will not remove mine integrity from me" (Job 27:5). He is also on record in Job 13:15 saying, "Though he slay me, yet will I trust in him: but I will maintain mine own ways before him." This experience probably would be too much for the average person, but God allowed it to happen to Job to measure his integrity in crisis and to prove his godly allegiance.

As mentioned earlier, most people in life will encounter some form of life crisis, whether it be in business, family or personal finances, marriage, or health. Have you ever had trouble so bad that you just didn't know what to do? Have you ever felt like giving up because life had become so difficult? If you have, don't feel like you're alone—so have many others. In times like this, it sometimes seems much easier to do wrong than to do right.

For the born-again believer in Christ, tests and trials are part of the process of being conformed to the image of Christ. Suffering is something we must all face, because we are the children of God. We must daily carry our crosses while casting all our cares on Him. In the midst of any test, trial, or hardship, we are tempted away from integrity in so many different ways. I've certainly have had my share of hardships and temptations.

In 1997, after serving twenty-one years of naval service, I underwent a family crisis where I experienced tremendous grief and loss. I lost a home, automobile, wife, and four small children through domestic dispute and marital dissension. I didn't anticipate having to go through spousal separation, child support, and eventually divorce. I encountered thoughts and feelings I didn't know existed; I felt disappointed by God, and I experienced things I never imagined I would ever experience. I remember the days and months I spent crying, trying to figure out why these things were happening. I felt like God had abandoned me, that He had left me for dead. But somewhere deep inside of me, I knew He didn't. At some point it became a matter of survival and not self-pity. I was having to start my life over at forty-one, even entering naval retirement earlier than intended.

Late one evening as I was driving to a store, thinking and crying along the way, I came to a four-way stop where I just laid my head on the steering wheel and cried with great emotion. Suddenly, I heard a voice say to me, "I still love you." I knew it was the voice of God, and I found a strength to lift my head in hope. A few days later as I knelt in prayer, God said to me, "Let it go." I then realized that I could no longer change what was happening to me, and that I should focus on what was before me. Regardless of how difficult it was, I recognized it was the best thing to do. I often admonish others to not look through metaphorical rearview mirrors unless looking to see how good, merciful, and kind God has been, and how far he has brought them. A few years later, I relocated to my home State of Louisiana, moved in with my parents for a short season as I recovered from the deep personal losses, reembarked on my path to finish college, began working a full-time job, and remarried. Two years later, I was called to pastor a small church while still working my secular job. Seven years later, my employer released me, and I became a full-time pastor. Everything that happened to me seemed like a setup by God that ushered me further into my purpose.

I taught a message on surviving hard places. In that message, I attempted to show the hearer the common element of hard places and how to face challenges as they occur. I defined a hard place as somewhere you feel that the necessary knowledge, wisdom, resource, or ability to recover and move forward from a situation doesn't exist. It is a place where you don't know what to do when realizing something must be done. It is a place where you know what is desired or required but lack the wherewithal to get it done. Regardless of the crisis or hardship you may encounter, integrity must remain relevant in getting through tough times.

The Christian in particular should always be mindful of possessing integrity when being tested. God looks for our best in trials and tribulations, and it takes a problem, a crisis, bad situation, need, longing, or even an enemy to prove our faith and integrity. Integrity in crisis, or possessing hardship integrity does not permit us to take shortcuts or circumvent processes. For instance, if you've lost your job, you don't become a bank robber to survive. If your spouse cheats on you or if something has negatively affected your marriage, don't seek to get back at them. If you're single and having a hard time sexually, don't become promiscuous in order to survive the hardship. There is a biblical standard to uphold as Christians. In Psalm 25:21, David said these words, "Let integrity and uprightness preserve me; for I wait on thee." There are many Scriptures to help us during times of crisis and hardship of every sort, so I encourage prayer and the Word of God to help strengthen, guide, and comfort everyone in God's grace. Galatians 6:9 says, "And let us not be weary in well doing: for in due season we shall reap, if we faint not." My advice to anyone is never quit on integrity.

Stress is physical, mental, or emotional strain or tension resulting from a situation, occurrence, or factor, and people handle stress in different ways. For some people, suicide is the ultimate escape from stress. Christians should always remember that God loves and cares about them, and it is not His will that anyone commit suicide, nor take the life of another individual who may have caused personal grief.

Stress occurs when we feel an imbalance between a problem or challenge, and the resources we have to deal with them.

Here are a few things to consider when experiencing crisis or facing hardship and pain:

- Look for joy through the optimistic lens of faith and hope. James 1:2 says to consider it all joy when you fall into various tests, trials, and temptations. Doing so will give you something to look forward to. You may cry for a season, but you won't cry forever.
- God knows how much you can bear; therefore, He won't allow any more than your capacity, measure or ability to be placed upon you. There is always an end, a way out, a means of bearing what you may be suffering. Always say to yourself, "There's enough grace for this problem."
- You are never alone. Always know that God will never leave or forsake you, even though you may feel differently. Trust God with all of your heart while trying hard to not rely on personal feelings and emotions as the right response.
- Bad experiences have a tendency of making some people bitter and unhappy. If you have taken a path toward the worst, stop! If not,

you may blame others for not being able to be happy, and a negative culture may remain part of your life.

- Determine your needs, and create a plan to meet those needs, tweaking as necessary.

- Cease castigating yourself for every disappointment occurring in your past. Certainly, there is a place for personal accountability, but always blaming yourself should have no place going forward in any recovery. Forgive and love yourself while also forgiving others.

- You can forgive someone for a wrong and still feel the pain of that wrong. Does that mean you have not forgiven them? No, it may mean you just have to move on and be healed, which should occur.

- Always try to avoid living in the memory of an experience that recreates the pain, or a memory that refuses to let the pain die.

- Pray always. In every challenge, particularly where hard decisions must be made, seek guidance through prayer to God, and He will answer your prayers to direct you.

- Exercise patience throughout each transitional phase or season. Don't try to make everything right in one day; it won't happen.

- Surround yourself with positive people, not finger pointers, fault finders, accusers, or pessimists. This may be difficult when desiring someone to share your pain with, who understands what you're going through. It's always better to associate yourself with those who are unbiased about your complaint and feelings of disheartenment.

- Include integrity into every life changing thought, decision and action. Avoid making life altering decisions when you're angry and disgusted with someone or about something. Your reasoning and rationale may not be clear during these times, and you may do something you'll regret later.

This is not an exhaustive list of considerations, but they provide a good place to start when dealing with crises and hardships. For all of God's children, particularly those who put their trust in Him, and regardless of what they're facing in life, God gives this assurance in Isaiah 43:2 that when you pass through the rising waters of life, God is there with you; when you find yourself wading through murky rivers, they won't overflow you; when you walk through fiery situations, you will not be burned, and the flame will not ignite upon you. Be encouraged.

When moving on from a bad and painful experience, be ready to answer the person you've become.

CHAPTER SEVEN

Friendship and Brotherly Integrity

Have you ever been violated in any manner by a friend or Christian brother? Have you ever violated in any manner a friend or Christian brother? The answer might be yes for both questions. In this chapter I would like to challenge us to become better friends and brothers to our friends and brothers. While this may not seem very important to some readers, you may be alarmed at the number of relationships that have been torn apart because of a lack of integrity. I often say, "If you haven't yet experienced a certain teaching or discussion point, keep living; eventually you might."

A friend will always love you, regardless of the circumstances, and a true brother is born for adversity (Proverbs 17:17). Brother in this context has a wider sense of literal relationship and metaphorical affinity, and is not restricted to a sibling relationship. This Scripture provides great comfort and assurance for those who have genuine friend and brother relationships. In today's vernacular, the words *friend* and *brother* are closely related, because for some, to have a friend is to have a brother. However, among many men, *brother* seems to be the word of choice. Many females tend to use the word *friend* or *sister* when referring to another female in close association, but in either case, there is not much difference between parties in close relationship.

Jesus gives a provoking message when describing a certain friendship in Luke 11:5-8 (KJV):

> And he said unto them, Which of you shall have a friend, and shall go unto him at midnight, and say unto him, Friend, lend me three loaves; For a friend of mine in his journey is come to me, and I have nothing to set before him? And he from within shall answer and say, Trouble me not: the door is now shut, and my children are with me in bed; I cannot rise and give thee. I say unto you, Though he will not rise and give him, because he is his friend, yet because of his importunity he will rise and give him as many as he needeth.

From this particular illustration, it is clear that being a friend carries with it a great deal of responsibility. No person should fear going to a friend, especially in a time of need. Now imagine that if the friend who was already in bed refused to oblige his pleading friend. Would you still consider him a friend? Would you feel the friendship had been breached or negatively affected? The responses to these questions will vary depending on how individuals define their personal relationships. I believe in most friendships, there is an element of understanding another person's position in awkward situations, and where friendships remain strong. However, there are situations when it may be difficult to forgive the offense of a friend. And even if forgiveness is granted, the relationship may never be the same.

A friend or brother does not wish to hurt the feelings of another friend or brother when the intent is for the good. For instance, there is a guy dating a woman with a bad reputation that he does not know about. Those who are aware of her reputation won't say anything to him about it because they believe it isn't their concern. Others may avoid saying anything because they don't want to discourage the guy, or they fear retaliation by the woman. However, the guy has a friend or brother in the Lord who loves him and does not want to see him hurt, so he brings the matter about the woman to his friend's attention, even risking that it may hurt him or that he may reject it as a lie if he has deep feelings for her. This is another good example of having integrity as a friend or brother. What would you do if this were your friend or brother?

Trust is a major part of integrity among friends. When there are difficult decisions to be made between two people, trust must be factored into the equation. Proverbs 27:6 says, "Faithful are the wounds of a friend; but the kisses of an enemy are deceitful." A person of integrity will rarely have a friend or brother who has no integrity in the relationship. In relationships where much personal and sensitive information is shared, having integrity is very important. When integrity has been breached between friends and brothers, trust is usually lost and the relationship may become severed beyond repair. However, everything, even repairing broken relationships, is possible through the power of God's love.

Integrity rarely seems relevant to some people until they are on the receiving end of a friendship or situation that has gone wrong.

Friendship Betrayals

To be hurt by a friend is a gut-twisting experience that could lead to two people becoming totally estranged from each other, though they once walked in close company and felt they knew each other. Friend betrayals take on various forms. You may ask, why is this important? Isn't it a part of life? Yes, it is a part of life, but it is also important that the household of God's children know how to handle friend betrayals when they occur. After all, there should be distinguishable differences in how Christians handle friend betrayals as compared to how unbelievers handle them. I have certainly had experiences on both sides, and I can tell you, it's not the same. Before I was born again, if a supposedly trusted friend betrayed our friendship, they would not be my close friend any longer, and there would usually be some contention.

I had an experience when unsaved wherein a close Navy friend of mine told a female about comments I had made about her. My friend and I often sat around playing cards and drinking together. When she heard about the comments, she stormed into my barracks and began knocking furiously at my room door. When I opened the door to greet her, she upsettingly expressed her displeasure at comments I made about her. She had every right to be upset because we were all friends and knew each other well. I tried to defend myself, but to no avail. Afterwards, I went to see my male friend about his actions, and he apologized, but my trust in him was damaged, and I never again got very personal with him after the incident. He felt uncomfortable when in my company at nightclubs and elsewhere. At the beginning, I told him I was going to get back at him for what he did, but I never retaliated; it would have made matters worse. I am certain that many of you have also had experiences of betrayal as a friend, either as the offender, or the person being offended.

When thinking of betrayals, one of the most popular literary phrases written in British literature, from Shakespeare's *Julius Caesar*, comes to mind: "Et tu, Brute?" This is Latin for "Even you, Brutus?" This play was one of my favorite readings when I was in school. This phrase was said in the scene where Julius Caesar is being assassinated. During this scene, Caesar recognizes his friend Marcus Brutus as one of the assassins. An unexpected betrayal by a friend is painful. King David said in Psalms 41:9, "Yea, mine own familiar friend, in whom I trusted, which did eat of my bread, hath lifted up his heel against me." From this we can learn that people do have the potential to betray, but this does not mean that every friend will. When it does happen, all you might think about is how much you shared, and how much they knew about you as a friend. David also wrote in Psalm 55:12-14:

> For it was not an enemy that reproached me; then I could have borne it: neither was it he that hated me that did magnify himself against me; then I would have hid myself from him: But it was thou, a man mine equal, my guide, and mine acquaintance. We took sweet counsel together, and walked unto the house of God in company.

As you can see from David's experience, being a believer does not exempt anyone from being betrayed by those with whom they've had close ties.

When we consider Jesus Christ and His betrayal by the disciple Judas Iscariot, certainly it was ordained by God that Jesus would be betrayed by Judas Iscariot to be crucified. But think about how the other disciples may have felt when finding out that one of their brothers was a traitor. In John 15:15 Jesus called the disciples His friends if they did what He commanded them.

Some of the most difficult betrayals to overcome are those committed by family members.

The question for us today is, how hard is it for us to handle being betrayed by a friend or brother? Do we harbor unforgiveness? Do we retaliate against them? Do we separate ourselves from them to never speak again? Do we broadcast their wrongdoing to every other believer? There are biblical instructions on how we can keep ourselves in integrity, even after being betrayed and hurt. Christ is the perfect example to the church. He teaches us to forgive those who trespass against us. In the Gospel of Matthew 18:15, Jesus is on record saying, "Moreover if thy brother shall trespass against thee, go and tell him his fault between thee and him alone: if he shall hear thee, thou hast gained thy brother." He teaches us the way of love. In Luke 6:27 Jesus replies, "But I say unto you which hear, Love your enemies, do good to them which hate you." You might be struggling to do that right now because of some existing pain, but for your own personal well-being, you must try. Betrayals are like any other offense between two individuals. In James 5:16, James writes, "Confess your faults one to another, and pray one for another, that ye may be healed. The effectual fervent prayer of a righteous man availeth much." For many Christians, this is one of the most difficult Scriptures to apply because of the associated guilt, shame, and pain of having to confess a wrong, particularly a fault of betrayal.

In many situations, the person causing pain through betrayal may not only be a friend, it might also be a relative, a spouse, or a partner. You may have been cheated on, abused physically and emotionally, etc., or you may have been the one who committed such offense against another, but in either case, there is healing and forgiveness in God, and we must forgive each other. Jesus says in Matthew 6:14-15, "For if ye forgive men their trespasses, your heavenly Father will also forgive you: But if ye forgive not men their trespasses, neither will your Father forgive your trespasses."

One of the most fascinating scriptural experiences of betrayal, other than that of Jesus by Judas, is the betrayal Joseph experienced by his brothers, who were the sons of Jacob, named Israel, one of the twelve patriarchs of the tribes of Israel. The story is chronicled in Genesis 37-50. Of all his sons, Israel loved his youngest son Joseph most because he was the son of his old age. Because of this, the other sons hated Joseph and would not speak kindly to him. To make matters worse, Joseph dreamed dreams that indicated he would have some form of reign or authority over his brothers, even over his parents. Though Israel, his father, rebuked his son, he considered Joseph's dreams—but that didn't change anything with Joseph's brothers. They eventually thought of a wicked scheme to get rid of Joseph by putting him into a pit without water, leaving him to die, and telling their father that an evil beast devoured him. They took his "coat of many colors" (Genesis 37:23) and dipped it in animal blood as "evidence" of his death, then gave the coat to their father. Merchants from Midian came along, pulled Joseph from the pit alive, and sold him to the descendants of Ishmael. They took him to Egypt where he was sold to Potiphar, an officer of Pharaoh and captain of the guard.

Joseph was exalted in Potiphar's house, but he encountered adversity, including imprisonment, because of a false accusation by Potiphar's wife. Even while he was in prison, God's favor remained with Joseph. After two years, Pharaoh dreamed a dream that Joseph then interpreted, and Joseph was exonerated and exalted by Pharaoh to govern his house and all the affairs of Egypt, with no one ruling over Joseph but Pharaoh. For seven years, Joseph gathered crops in advance of a famine, and when the famine finally came, no one had food except for the Egyptians. As governor, he sold corn to countries who came to Egypt to buy food.

Because of the famine, Joseph's brothers and his father also came from Canaan to Egypt to buy corn, but Joseph did not immediately reveal himself to them. Eventually, though, he did. He was glad to see his father again, and to see his brother Benjamin, the son of Rachel; his father and brothers, all coming to Egypt.

Israel, their father, later died, and Joseph's brothers who did the evil against him probably assumed he would retaliate against them for the evil they did unto him, but Joseph in Genesis 50:20 said, "But as for you, ye thought evil against me; but God meant it unto good, to bring to pass, as it is this day, to save much people alive." Joseph demonstrated love, forgiveness, and compassion toward his brothers when it would have seemed easy to be vindictive against them. What an amazing response and great example of brotherly integrity in the face of betrayal.

Because you're a man or woman of God, you'll also do the right things, even if the other refuses. Therefore, let your integrity guide you through the painful season of being betrayed by a partner, friend, brother, relative, or spouse. In doing so, God is represented and honored with your integrity as a Christian.

CHAPTER EIGHT

Ministry Integrity

A minister's integrity empowers them to preach and teach God's word with a pure conscience.

Ministry integrity is being breached in the body of Christ, but restoring ministry integrity begins with personal integrity. Unless an individual is called by God, is capable of presenting Christ through personal integrity and testimony, is anointed of the Holy Ghost, and understands the will of God given to them, they should not be considered ready for leading a ministry. Individuals who are not ready are admonished to wait on their ministry, according to Romans 12:6-7. I believe this gives each ministry candidate sufficient time to study Scripture, become established in prayer, and understand the will of God. Most often, these individuals serve under already established ministries and leaders in some capacity as they grow in wisdom, knowledge, and experience. Most people going forth into ministry are recognized and confirmed by God through some form of presbyterial order, by the office of a bishop or ranking clergy, and by the laying on of hands. This sending forth should not be done without proper confirmation of the Holy Ghost, but in some occurrences, this confirmation appears to be made through human criteria of the flesh;

e.g., a large financial donor, nepotism, or some other carnal basis, none of which are true qualifiers for leading a ministry.

Many people started off in ministry with good intentions of serving God with integrity, but through lust of the flesh and the pride of life, many have also become deceived and gone astray, even while still possessing ministry titles and positions. It is time to take a stand against the lack of integrity that has infiltrated mostly every venue where ministry works are conducted, endeavoring to restore Christian virtues and values back into the Christian culture.

Certainly, God gives us grace, but He also requires a righteous way of thinking, a safeguarding attitude and response, that we might be well-pleasing to Him. There are many things Scripture warns us about so that we might have and retain ministry integrity, and in this discourse, I will highlight some of the most glaring concerns.

Satan is after that which is holy, the church institution, and has publicly desecrated it, particularly through television programs where actors literally blaspheme the name of Jesus. There is a religious system with a voice that attempts to shut out the voice of truth, particularly through those who hold positions of authority and leadership in churches and ministries. The message has moved away from Christ, toward each man for himself. Many who were once considered humble, faithful, and true have become idolatrous in behavior with attitudes of discontentment and greed.

There is a covert operation, a satanic network of false preachers, operating in the world that has disguised and embedded its operations under the church name. This satanic spirit is doing all it can to release the character of Barabbas, an unrepentant personality, a notable felon, who the crowd wanted released by Pilate when he asked them, "... Whom will ye that I release unto you? Barabbas, or Jesus which is called Christ? ... They said, Barabbas (Matthew 27:16-21). Unfortunately, there are many people today who prefer to see the persecution of the name of Jesus Christ and all that He taught. Many evangelical pastors and church leaders have compromised the truth of God's character to embrace ungodly political ideologies and personalities that are unrepresentative of God's way.

The church must remain united on every issue of life where Christ is represented.

Ministry integrity involves every believer. Ministry service includes every task carried out in God's will, whether as an usher, musician, evangelist, pastor, or other position. Integrity must abide in the heart as the ambassadors of Christ. Proverbs 4:23 states, "Keep thy heart with all diligence; for out of it are the issues of life." As we understand it, every ministry worker must have a constant guard around the heart when doing ministry, because the devil seeks to undermine the things representative of the Kingdom of God on earth, and the believer is the instrument the devil seeks to tarnish so that the name of Jesus is also tarnished. Once the heart has become corrupted with fleshly ambitions and distractions that affect how the worker does ministry, ministry is not being presented in its purest form. The apostle Paul writes in 2 Corinthians 6:3-4 that as ministry workers, we should not give offense in any part of what we do for Christ so that the ministry is not accused or at fault, but that we should approve ourselves as the ministers of God, with much patience, in afflictions, in necessities, in distresses, and in many other things Paul mentioned in this chapter. He further writes in 2 Corinthians 4:1-2:

Therefore seeing we have this ministry, as we have received mercy, we faint not; But have renounced the hidden things of dishonesty, not walking in craftiness, nor handling the word of God deceitfully, but by manifestation of the truth commending ourselves to every man's conscience in the sight of God.

If every actively-involved believer possessed a conviction that integrity was significant in church or ministry governance, I believe the general state of the Church would be greatly enhanced. But instead, the church institution has a diminished status, with many seeing it as a modern-day joke to be scoffed at. I can't imagine Christ being happy with this; neither should the members be happy with this. Unfortunately, Christianity suffers because of the broad negativity surrounding church ministry and Christian conduct. I've spoken with and have seen many believers who are totally frustrated with the games, entertainment, and lack of seriousness from those confessing to be saints of God and ministry workers. Some prefer to stay home during regular worship times, while some prefer small group meetings in homes and makeshift gathering places, while others just don't attend church at all. What has become a popular trend among many believers is watching worship services via a live-stream on computers, phones, and other electronic devices, in order to avoid putting up with the counterfeit and deceitful behaviors found in some church environments. It's also a convenience to observe a live church service from the comfort of one's home. Certainly, there is no real tradeoff value for not being part of an actual worship experience with other Christians. However, a lot of Christians are only interested in one or two activities of a worship service, and giving financially is not one of them.

A major threat against the ministry integrity of the church also comes from those who identify with it, who are familiar with its rituals, attitudes, dogmas, and common expressions, but who present another form of Christ to draw men away from the common faith to themselves. Jesus said in Matthew 7:15, "Beware of false prophets, which come to you in sheep's clothing, but inwardly they are ravening wolves." The Greek translation for ravening means *rapacious*, which is to seize for plunder or the satisfaction of greed; a person who is like this is considered an extortioner, a robber. I have seen this demonic work in churches. Jesus goes on to further explain in the seventh chapter of Matthew how these extortioners could be identified by their fruits, even saying that not everyone who pretends in worship or calls upon the Lord will access the kingdom of heaven; only those who do the will of the Father which is in heaven. John 4:24 plainly states that God, as Spirit, must be adored and worshipped with spiritual integrity and truth. Beloved, the Scripture plainly warns us of these ungodly actions in ministry.

Let's look at a key playground where the devil circulates and disperses its venomous activities: *social media*. Some people are using social media to cast negativity upon the church and the reputation of Christians, particularly those who are well-known in ministry circles. I believe this plays right into the strategy of the devil to defame the name of Jesus Christ. Everyone makes mistakes or commits errors in judgment. There are a countless number of internet bloggers whose focus is to highlight the human frailty of a Christian who has allegedly done something that they themselves don't have all the details about, and this behavior contributes to dividing the members of the body of Christ. As Christians, let's endeavor to restore the integrity of love and forgiving one another. The body of Christ must pray for each other, not publicizing every misstep of another member of the body of Christ as though they themselves have never committed a wrong. Proverbs 17:9 states, "He that covereth a transgression seeketh love; but he that repeated a matter separateth [very] friends."

Many individuals, churches, and ministries have used websites and applications to create and share content; e.g. daily spiritual encouragement, scriptural analysis, notice of upcoming events, sermons, music, and much more to the good of the church body. However, many have exploited it to promulgate falsehood and misleading Christian ideologies, all in the name of Jesus Christ. Transmitting distorted messages of God for personal attention, fame, or fortune has become a modern social medial trend that embellishes the Word of God and the name of Jesus with false characterizations and fictitious overlays. It is often prominent and well-known ministry personalities who seize this platform for selfish reasons such as personal acclaim, mostly drawing those who don't know God or Scripture well enough to discern truth from a lie. These slick personalities seek to promote themselves as godly figures to be trusted, typifying the ruthless ambition of devils sent to destroy the integrity of Jesus' name. It is too easy to be fooled over social media these days. The beloved disciple John wrote in one of his epistles, "Beloved, believe not every spirit, but try the spirits whether they are of God: because many false prophets are gone out into the world" (1 John 4:1).

These men and women have crossed lines to become popular and to reach celebrity status in the Church ministry. They prey upon the blind. They use their skills in ministry for entertainment and to receive attention for their gifts. They mislead through earthly philosophy and doctrines of men. They seduce the weak, bruised, hurt, and disappointed; those who need someone to trust or are looking for some type of confirmation, comfort, and consolation. These are wolves in sheep's clothing; men who by their conduct damage others morally; who sit in our feast of worship and praise to God who don't promote godly integrity, only their hidden agendas. They often speak fast with charismatic gestures to attract one's attention to style and not to substance. They declare that every lifestyle is acceptable for salvation on behalf of grace and Christian love, while scrutinizing those who have taken a stance on upholding godly integrity and righteous living standards.

While leading up to one of his final missionary trips and being warned of impending trouble, the apostle Paul said to pastors, overseers, and ministry leaders, as recorded in Acts 20:28-31:

Take heed therefore unto the yourselves, and to all the flock, over the which the Holy Ghost had made you overseers, to feed the Church of God, which he hath purchased with his own blood. For I know this, that after my departing shall grievous wolves enter in among you, not sparing the flock. Also of your own selves shall men arise, speaking perverse things, to draw away disciples after them. Therefore watch, and remember, that by the space of three years I ceased not to warn every one night and day with tears.

Being part of this generation of Church and ministry overseers, I admonish each of us to keep this tenet of governance over our churches. Also, as an admonishment to the true ministers of the grace of God, if we're going to use social media to reach the masses for Christ, let's tell the truth. Deception is high across various ministry outlets, and it will get worse as the return of Christ draws near.

Under no circumstances should anyone, particularly a Christian, breach integrity just to have a friend.

Integrity is also breached when the ministry worker is more concerned about being liked and well-spoken of in the church and community. Jesus was despised and rejected; the prophets were slain; the early apostles and Christians were often beaten, imprisoned, and martyred for the gospel's sake and for their testimony of Christ, but many of today's ministry workers are more concerned about others liking them. Some people will become anybody to be liked by somebody. In Luke's gospel, Jesus is on record saying, "Woe unto you, when all men shall speak well of you! for so did their fathers to the false prophets" (Luke 6:26). Quite frankly, I don't believe anyone living in a godly manner, who testifies the truth of God with the authority of the Holy Spirit, will have a lot of good things said about them by the world, and even by some who confess Jesus Christ as Savior.

Ministry work, and the worker also, must be confined to a circumference of holiness and true righteousness, but most importantly, love must be at the center of everything done in the name of Jesus. 1 Corinthians 13 summarizes it best, so I encourage every believer to become familiar with this chapter, and to know how significant charity is in ministry.

Grace is not a permit to be or do the things we imagine, think, or feel are right as long as a majority agrees with it.

Nepotism

Let's look at how nepotism affects a church's health.

Nepotism is very popular in today's churches. Many pastors of very large congregations put their children or other relatives in key ministry positions as a precursor to them becoming the next leaders of the church. I strongly believe that children of pastors should be actively involved in ministry support functions and prepared to assume greater responsibility. It is a blessing to have them in the church. However, not every child of a pastor will meet the qualifications of leadership. Even the sons of the good kings of Judah and Israel proved that nepotism does not always work favorably, as some did not follow after God as their fathers did before them.

Preferential treatment on the basis of family relationships should not be condoned in the Churches of Jesus Christ.

Using nepotistic patterns to run a church can create hostility between relatives and other workers when not properly monitored. There was a situation in a church where a woman loved the Lord and enjoyed serving in the music ministry, but the pastor's wife consistently acted in a manner unrepresentative of Christian character toward the woman. The pastor's wife appeared jealous and often bitter toward the woman; never having anything good to say about her. The really sad part is that both served in the music department. The woman was highly gifted and anointed, and the congregation was often inspired and joyed by her anointed singing, but there was a rift between the woman and the pastor's wife that the two women could not resolve on their own, even though friends often encouraged the woman. Some music ministry workers admonished her to be loving and strong, but avoided any direct involvement between the two women. Eventually, someone advised her to counsel with the pastor if they could not resolve the dispute, seeing it was the pastor's wife involved. The woman followed the advice and counseled with the pastor concerning his wife's behavior toward her. When departing the session, she felt good, and believed the pastor would bring them together to discuss the situation for resolution, but instead, the pastor used the discussion in a sermon to berate or scold the woman, but without calling her by name. Everyone familiar with the situation knew who the rebuke was intended for. The woman was so hurt and devastated by the experience that she later left the church, much to the chagrin of those who enjoyed her contribution to the ministry. Unfortunately, other congregants witnessed the pastor's wife involved in similar situations with other women in the church. This is a true illustration of nepotism, where the pastor's wife received favorable treatment because of her relationship with the pastor.

There may be places where some family members believe they have ministry rights and privileges above that of other members of a congregation, but unfair and unethical behaviors as believers toward others should not be tolerated in the houses of God. As a Christian, I understand how important it is to have ministry integrity in all ministry functions. There are situations of nepotism in churches that damage unity among its members, and this cannot be condoned. Philippians 2:3 says, "Let nothing be done through strife or vainglory; but in lowliness of mind let each esteem other better than themselves." Doing this will eliminate anyone behaving inappropriately toward any member of the body of Christ.

Jesus made it clear that family relationships had no bearing on His ministry or how He interacted with people. Matthew 12:46-50 describes a conversation Jesus had as He talked to the people. Someone apparently pointed out to Him that His mother and brothers were waiting to talk with Him. Jesus responded, "Who is my mother? And who are my brothers?" He further replied, "For whosoever shall do the will of my Father which is in heaven, the same is my brother, sister, and mother" (Matthew 12:50). It would probably be difficult for some pastors and church leaders to take a position like this without feeling the displeasure of a family member, especially one that seeks preferential treatment as a worker in the ministry because they are related.

Gain and Riches

One of the major breaches of integrity in ministry comes through the temptation of *gain and riches*. An argument heard all throughout Christian communities is that God wants us to prosper, even as our soul prospers, and be in good health, with which I totally agree. I have met ministers of the gospel who have stated that they're seeking to become rich; they're trying to reach the top. Let me reiterate, I believe God wants to prosper people financially, particularly the children of God. However, there is a certain scriptural caution we must embrace when desiring financial gain and riches. 1 Timothy 6:9 states, "But they that will be rich fall into temptation and a snare, and into many foolish and hurtful lusts, which drown men in destruction and perdition." Paul goes on further to say, "Charge them that are rich in this world, that they be not high-minded, nor trust in uncertain riches, but in the living God, who giveth us richly all things to enjoy" (1 Timothy 6:17).

Let me be clear, this is not a narrative against wealth. But, as previously stated, there are clear warnings about ungodly and improper attitudes concerning gain and riches. Proverbs 23:4 admonishes us by saying, "Labor not to be rich: cease from thine own wisdom." Psalm 62:10 reminds us that if our financial status improves to being wealthy, we should not set our hearts upon this wealth. This has been the danger for so many Christian believers. It's a topic that is approached from one aspect when discussing it: We need money, and God wants us to have it. However, some people are never satisfied, and subsequently they plow headlong into destructive habits, forsaking even the thought of integrity. Therefore, the Christian must be guarded against destructive behaviors associated with riches, and gain; seeking foremost to be rich toward God.

Acquiring a strong resistance to this temptation begins with a controlled attitude. Proper reasoning usually involves answering tough questions internally to help guide behaviors. Such is the case with every type of temptation of the flesh, but primarily with money, because it is that which we must have, and having much of it seems to be the desired goal.

A controlled attitude is an attitude that is governed by proper reasoning concerning a subject, matter, or issue.

There are some who will go to great lengths to satisfy a longing, and it appears that many Christians are just as much out of control in a quest to be rich as the worldly are. Ecclesiastes 10:19 states, "A feast is made for laughter, and wine maketh merry: but money answereth all things."

A gentleman once commented about a 2008 Chevrolet Trailblazer that I drive, stating I was under-representing the role of a pastor. I was shocked at the statement. Certainly, I don't see anything wrong with the vehicle, and will continue to drive it. I'm grateful to have it as much as the other vehicles. It has a polished, clean, white exterior with leather interior, sunroof, and chrome wheels. If I drove a Maserati, Rolls-Royce, or some other expensive, high-end vehicle, he may have said something to the contrary. When Paul addressed the church at Philippi and their desire to bless him, he said, ". . . for I have learned, in whatsoever state I am, therewith to be content" (Philippians 4:11). This is a difficult mindset for many Christians.

It was once said to me that a pastor would come to his regular worship services in expensive cars and fine clothing, and wearing costly jewelry, but the church could barely pay its mortgage, the building was in need of repairs, and many of the church members were having financial difficulties. To many observers this would appear problematic. *Certainly, it is unfair to fault a pastor, ministry leader, or anyone for being financially successful, espe-*

cially when retiring from secular employment of many years. Many people are quick to assume that all pastors and ministry leaders are robbing church finances for personal gain, but this assumption is not true. Paul expressly stated in 1 Corinthians 9:11 as a church planter and overseer, "If we have sown unto spiritual things, is it a great thing if we shall reap your carnal things?" It is not uncommon or illegal to have compensation agreements for pastors, ministry leaders, and other church employees. However, it is not appropriate for a pastor or ministry leader to respond to their congregations by saying, "I have made mine, now let them make theirs." While this statement may have a tone of innocence, it also carries a slight tone of arrogance, and is not an acceptable position to hold for any pastor or ministry leader because, it lacks the Christ integrity of being concerned for the welfare of others. Unfortunately, a lot of people will evaluate the material aspects of churches to help them decide if they should become a covenant partner, give support, and in many situations, join a church. When a church or ministry focuses its teaching primarily on money and worldly riches, it is poised to attract the material-minded believer only, if standards of holiness and godly integrity are not also emphasized.

This topic of riches is so very important to Christian ministry because it is one of the biggest downfalls which destroys people and severs them from their ministries, to the point sometimes of imprisonment for wrongdoing such as mishandling ministry finances. Ministry organizations, pastors, and church administrators have a responsibility to ensure that accurate accounting protocols and governance are in place to prevent this. It is also important that financial contributions by donors, gifts to speakers, honorariums, and salaries of ministry workers are handled according to the highest standards of integrity to avoid theft, embezzlement, and other inappropriate activities that betray the trust of donors and contributors. This is significant in preserving the integrity of ministry applications and avoiding legal troubles for the Church or ministry. There are a number of resources, for example, nonprofit literature and books, online resources, accountants, and organized conferences, that offers a wealth of information, training, and assistance to help churches and ministries in the area of financial accountability and integrity.

God wants us to be more spiritual-minded than worldly-minded. He wants mankind to be born-again and filled with the Holy Ghost, having spiritual riches, as well as being financially prosperous. 1 Timothy 6:7 clearly states, "For we brought nothing into this world, and it is certain we can carry nothing out." Jesus also says, "For it is easier for a camel to go through a needle's eye, than for a rich man to enter into kingdom of God" (Luke 18:25). The disciples, upon hearing this, questioned who can be saved? But Jesus assured them that with God all things are possible, even though with men this is impossible. The essence of this scripture is for the believer to trust God with their riches when required to give, while sustaining a hold on eternal life through faith. He went on to explain to the disciples in Luke 18:29-30, ". . . There is no man that hath left house, or parents, or brethren, or wife, or children, for the kingdom of God's sake, Who shall not receive manifold more in this present time, and in the world to come life everlasting." The analogy Jesus makes should be understood.

For those who have financial abundance and are in a position to advise or educate others, whether through church, business, or social networking; endeavor to impact the lives of the financially deprived by suggesting the necessary tools, information, and education to combat poverty and improve living standards. It's simply not enough to meet for prayer meetings and conduct worship services, but neglect the poor among us. Proverbs 19:17 states, "He that hath pity upon the poor lendeth unto the LORD; and that which he hath given will he pay him again."

There are countless number of people who regularly give to churches and ministries to support their outreaches, but they themselves live from paycheck to paycheck, oftentimes taking from one credit card to pay the balance on another credit card, waiting for a financial miracle as purported by those making request of financial support for ministry programs and various outreaches. Seed time and harvest is a principle of God, and one that I participate in. There have also been many Christians who have consistently given tithes and offerings in support of local and televised church outreaches while believing in and supporting the principle of giving, but who died financially broke, primarily because no one instructed them in the principles of *wealth accumulation*.

> *The lack of financial education, support, intelligence, or ingenuity are causes of many financial disparities.*

As we can see, integrity in the Church and among believers concerning riches and gain is important. When asking God for financial prosperity, ask with the intent to do more for right reasons. James 4:3 says, "Ye ask, and receive not, because ye ask amiss, that ye may consume it upon your lusts." Ask for wisdom to avoid the pitfalls and snares associated with riches and gain. 1 Timothy 6:10 says, "For the love of money is the root of all evil: which while some coveted after, they have erred from the faith, and pierced themselves through with many sorrows." Therefore, we pray, God bless us to be a blessing with wisdom.

Gift Integrity

The Church is getting a bad rap through its own supporters and workers with the inappropriate or wrongful application of gifts. This is a complex topic with much controversy among believers and ministry workers.

We must first understand that gifts and callings are from God, regardless of how they are honed. John the Baptist, when questioned about Jesus said, ". . . A man can receive nothing, except it be given him from heaven" (John 3:27). Paul also writes in Romans 11:29, "For the gifts and callings of God are without repentance." With all of the hysteria and lack of understanding surrounding the use of gifts, it is the responsibility of every individual in ministry to possess *gift integrity*. There are natural gifts, and there are spiritual gifts. As a skilled keyboard player who has never taken a piano lesson, it is of God that I have natural musical ability. Because *my* ability was primarily used in church, it doesn't mean that every skilled pianist will play in the Christian genre. There are skilled classical, jazz, pop, folk music, and hip-hop musicians, and every gift is given by God. Rarely will a gifted musician not desire compensation, and one way to attract and keep a good musician is to offer an attractive compensation package. But what about the smaller church without a musician, that doesn't have the financial capacity to offer attractive compensation packages? Is God only concerned for the larger churches? Many musicians don't consider this and instead shop their talents to the most financially capable church without any regard for the will of God concerning their gift.

I have known musicians who wanted compensation that exceeded fair market rates, even exceeding that of the pastor. This is sheer greed, and many small churches are without musicians because of these demands. Let's face it, having a well-organized music ministry is vital to churches and ministries, but what happened to the days of seeking to be in the will of God with our gifts and callings? What happened to the integrity of being faithful to a church or ministry without being lured to move elsewhere for more money? What happened to the musician that says, "Wherever I am sent, I'm trusting that God will give grace through some means to support my call"?

One might argue that people who work in secular professions often change jobs for higher pay. While that may be true, doing the Lord's will entails pleasing God. I have never read in Scripture where the gifted and called of God held financial negotiations with God before they went out, or contracted financially with Him before serving His purpose. Certainly, there are travel, food, and lodging expenses when traveling abroad to serve, even daily living expenses for those in full time ministry, and discussions about these matters should be held accordingly. Honorariums are appropriate, when determined.

God is equitable, fair, and just to reward all kingdom labors, small and large, but there is a shifting away from kingdom agendas to satisfy personal agendas.

I recall an evangelist telling me about a week-long revival meeting he was called to preach in another state. He did not request or specify an honorarium amount prior to starting the revival. After five nights of ministering, the host church did not give him an honorarium, neither was there an open request for love donations, so the last night of service was dismissed without a mention of being a blessing to the evangelist. He told me that as people were greeting him and saying how much they were blessed by his ministry, many were putting money in his hand, which he stuffed in his pants and coat pockets as he continued conversing with them. After returning to his hotel room and removing his clothing, he remembered putting things in his pockets, so he removed them, and was surprised beyond expectation at how much the people had given him. This experience further demonstrated to him God's faithfulness, and teaches us to be more concerned about doing God's will than about how much money we can make doing it. The writer in Hebrews 6:10 says, "For God is not unrighteous to forget your work and labor of love, which ye have shewed toward his name, in that ye have ministered to the saints, and do minister."

When I was called to pastor a church, I advised the board of directors not to pay me anything for the first three months when deciding a salary. I didn't ask to pastor; God called and sent me. I have never made any request for financial compensation, but God yet provides for my every need. Care must be exercised by church governing officials to recognize hirelings, those whose only intent is to gain as much as they can financially, while seeking the next highest bidder for their services. It may be an old-fashioned ministry philosophy, but I believe it's the proper way of using a gift with humility and integrity.

Many believers, even some unsaved persons, are perplexed by the use of spiritual gifts. *Gifts are necessary and are ordained by God for the body of Christ to do effective ministry accordingly.* The apostle Paul wrote to the Church of Corinth concerning spiritual gifts. The first thing he says in the opening sentence of his letter in 1 Corinthians 12 is, "Now concerning spiritual gifts brethren, I would not have you ignorant." Wow, what an opener! He goes on further to explain the diversities and operations of spiritual gifts, making it absolutely clear that God works in all of them. With that understanding, why is there so much debate among churches concerning the proper application of gifts? Could it be that there is a lack of teaching and proper usage of gifts? Or, could it be that some believers are not Spirit-filled to understand the things of the Spirit? If a gift is not properly governed and administered, it paves the way for confusion and damage, neither of which are God's will. I will not be discussing in detail every gift operation, but will aim to raise awareness of *gift integrity*.

Paul writes in 1 Corinthians 12:8-11:

For to one is given by the Spirit the word of wisdom; to another the word of knowledge by the same Spirit; To another faith by the same Spirit; to another the gifts of healing by the same Spirit; To another the working of miracles; to another prophecy; to another discerning of spirits; to another divers kinds of tongues; to another the interpretation of tongues: But all these worketh that one and the selfsame Spirit, dividing to every man severally as he wills.

As you can see, there are several ways for Satan to infiltrate the church with hostile intent, because "God is not the author of confusion, but of peace, as in all churches of the saints" (1 Corinthians 14:33). Satan undermines the good of God to wreak confusion in many churches. The gifts of prophecy and tongues have become two of the breeding grounds for Satan to negatively influence some churches, particularly Pentecostal charismatic assemblies. If there is a truth, then there certainly is a lie. If there are legitimate operations, then there are illegitimate operations. If there are true prophets, there are also false prophets. If there are genuine tongues, then there are fabricated tongues. As previously mentioned, 1 John 4:1 says we should not believe every spirit but try them to see of what sort they are; whether they are from God or from Satan, because many deceitful teachers and prophets are out to deceive. If there was ever a time to watch and pray, it is now.

There are those who practice satanism and evil works, who have secretly transformed themselves to appear as men and women of God. I often tell people that spiritual gifts can be imitated to deceive people, but one thing deceivers cannot do is live holy lives.

Gifts are given to edify. Some have compromised gift integrity through emotional manipulations for that which does not glorify God. Tongues have become a misused gift among many charismatic believers. Many theologians teach that tongues have ceased and are no longer relevant in the modern Church. I don't support that teaching because my experience with speaking in an unknown tongue as the Spirit gives utterance is genuine and scripturally supported. Praying in the Spirit is a relevant part of spiritual growth, as written in Jude 1:20, "But ye, beloved, building up yourselves on your most holy faith, praying in the Holy Ghost." When I was initially filled with the Holy Ghost, a supernatural event occurred in my life and I spoke in tongues, which has become part of my daily prayer language. According to 1 Corinthians 14, whoever speaks in an unknown tongue edifies himself, but he that brings forth prophesy edifies the Church. When a believer genuinely prays in an unknown tongue, their spirit prays, but they don't understand what is being said—unless God gives them interpretation of the tongue or reveals something by revelation.

Integrity of tongues is compromised when believers disorderly interrupt worship services with speaking in tongues without an interpretation for edification. Ministers should not teach or pray extensively in tongues just to prove to others they are spiritual. For those who are unbelievers and unlearned, and even to some who believe, this is madness. I have known situations where people have gotten up and walked out of a service because of these occurrences. They have the appearance of being cultish. I have had others tell me they didn't believe it was the Holy Spirit. I have explained to many believers, specifically those with spiritual gifts, the significance of having *gift integrity*, and that integrity is gained and supported through humility, seeking God, and having scriptural knowledge. 1 Corinthians 14:40 says, "Let all things be done decently and in order."

There are many Christian songwriters and singers who are exceptionally gifted, who travel globally and appear on television, whose opinions and feelings are replacing some scriptural teachings. Many of the younger Christians, because of an artist's global appeal will follow that artist above obeying their pastors and the Word of God. The gifted artist may have good intentions in their music to encourage and inspire, but in some song lyrics the message is not always established in sound biblical doctrine, but instead in a neo-Christian culture where almost everything is acceptable. At some point, some artists begin to feel invincible because of having rock star popularity and status. God did not intend for bestowed ministry gifts and operations to not be mixed with gospel integrity. Many have left the foundational church teachings from whence they began their ministries because of cultural demands and a desire to be accepted, especially among peers. With many of the current generation of popular gospel artists, their opinions often influence those who see them as cultural icons of inspiration for their generation. It is great to have inspiration at every level, but the person inspiring with a gift must not be arrogantly puffed up. The gifted must be able to receive correction and instruction in righteousness when necessary. Christian music, as with the teaching of the Word of God, should not be modified to conform to generational demands and standards of worldly pleasure.

There is a satanic attempt to weaken the gospel message through Christian artistry and misleading lyrical content. It appears that some of the older, living trailblazers of gospel music have stood back to let another generation transform their music tradition into the wrong message and the wrong way of presenting Christ through music.

Christian music that incites the flesh to ungodly behavior lacks godly content integrity.

It is understood that music evolves in pattern and style, but Christ integrity should not be omitted from the Christian genre. Therefore, the alarm must be sounded to bring the attention of the Christian back to gift integrity where the message of Jesus Christ remains consistently relevant.

There are other ministry gifts given to believers that must always have integrity to be God-pleasing and effective. The key is to always remember who gave the gift, and for what purpose; to walk submissively and humbly in the sight of God. Believers should pray for wisdom and understanding of the gift, and never use a gift to impress or draw attention to self.

The Church of Jesus Christ must not allow deviating factions to be part of its culture, but many church leaders have turned their heads and closed their eyes to these conditions.

Christian broadcasts have also become a pipeline for everyone who can pay for airtime to spew venomous, misleading, and damnable doctrines. God wants the gospel preached all over the world, but this venue is proving to be very harmful, as well as very good. Certainly, there are those who are true and are doing great works for the Lord, but there are others who cannot be overlooked as liars and deceivers. As children of God, we are to defend the integrity of the doctrine of Jesus Christ in a truthful and respectful way, and never in a contentious manner.

Leadership Integrity

A Church or ministry without integrity is a recipe for disaster, and does not provide an adequate foundation for honest and effective leadership.

Every ministry leader, regardless of rank, should possess leadership integrity. Leadership is part of every organization on earth, and I do not intend to make this section a leadership doctrine, but to stress integrity in how we lead as ministers and workers in the Church. We must first recognize that God trusted us to be good stewards over his heritage, and good leadership is the sum of many elements, not just one. Leadership must center around purpose, mission, goals, and objectives for accomplishment, and each element should be executed with integrity.

Throughout our lives working with different professional organizations, we understand the significance of leadership. Unfortunately, we've experienced the good, the bad, and the ugly. Oftentimes, a disgruntled employee is not always disgruntled about wages, but about dishonest leadership from decision makers, supervisors, and those setting the tone for how things are to be accomplished. This is what establishes the culture.

In some instances, heads of department are never around to see how things really are in the actual work environment because they rely on the information provided to them from intermediate level supervisors. However, I knew of a work situation where operations were being conducted but had no appointed supervisor present. The department head and other staff members, which were located at a separate building, rarely made visits to this particular workspace. Fortunately, the workers executed their jobs as required by standard operating procedures, but there were also times when there was confusion over certain procedural issues and other matters, which is not an uncommon occurrence in many work environments. Because there was no supervisory presence, workplace tension and strife also existed. There were times when some employees showed up late to work, while some took extended breaks and lunches. A properly structured leadership system would have an appointed supervisor or leader available to ensure organizational and operational integrity in the workplace. In this particular work situation there is no legitimate way of recognizing and rewarding stellar work performances, nor of reprimanding or counseling underperforming employees. Some employees resigned from their employment primarily for those reasons. Bad leadership may cause many employees to seek other employment opportunities.

Good ministry leadership, like any other organization, should not be performed with bias, especially being a Christian organization. For the Church, leadership must be executed with righteousness. Here are four basic Christian leadership considerations:

▶ *Christian leaders should lead as servants.* I've come to learn that those being led appreciate a leader who does not mind being part of a process or solution from a servant's perspective and not from a master's perspective; that is, do as I say, not as I do. Jesus said to His disciples that if any of them wanted to be great, chief, or first, they are to do it as a servant (Mark 10:44).

▶ *Leaders cannot be afraid of obeying God when others disagree with God.* Christian leaders should have exceptional spiritual bearings. This is important when called to lead as the Spirit of God directs. There are many supporters of Christ who prefer that a leader not be a compromiser of godly standards when leading. Leaders should seek God's way, especially when faced with great challenges. Leaders must obey God or suffer negative consequences.

▶ *Leaders should always treat others as they would desire to be treated if the situation were reversed.* When love for the people is demonstrated, more is accomplished. Proverbs 29:2 says, "When the righteous are in authority, the people rejoice: but when the wicked beareth rule, the people mourn." I am constantly evaluating my leadership habits to ensure that I am performing them with a Christ-like integrity. *Positional authority, which is authority conferred upon by appointment, does not necessarily make anyone a good Christian leader.*

▶ *Christian leaders should have daily prayer that includes prayers for wisdom and knowledge.* It is so important to know God's will through prayer. A Christian leader cannot be effective without prayer. We live in a time when ministry leaders have a "cut and copy" approach to doing ministry. In other words, do it like someone else is doing it. I think this is a dangerous habit for a leader because God has to order each leader's step. Imitating good habits is a plus for any Christian leader, but caution must be exercised when trying to imitate everything else someone is doing.

There are many pastors with small congregations trying to function as a megachurch in a season when they're still wearing diapers or in a kindergarten season of ministry. This is ill-advised. Oftentimes, the pressure to do this begins with well-established church leaders who make public statements as though the church pastor with a small congregation is irrelevant. It becomes a self-imposed pressure when the small church leader unfairly compares their congregation size with larger church congregations. The writer in Ecclesiastes, believed to be King Solomon, spoke about a poor wise man who by his wisdom delivered a small city where only a few men lived when the city came under siege by a great king who had built strong bulwarks against it. He went on to say that the poor man's wisdom was despised and his words were not heard (Ecclesiastes 9:14-16). I say to every pastor with only a few people to shepherd, don't be intimidated and don't move away from the work God has given you. Don't misinterpret God's instructions to you. Don't put the church in bad debt just to appear as a growing ministry to others. Until God gives the next instruction, keep doing the current instruction. This is another way of maintaining leadership integrity.

When I was first sent to pastor a church, it was an awkward feeling, because I had become a non-denominational preacher being sent to a denominational church. I have a Pentecostal denominational background because that's the culture I grew up in after being filled with the Holy Spirit, but that's not the same culture I was sent to pastor. When I was called to pastor, God had already weaned me away from denominational thinking, which is not a denial of my Pentecostal root. As you might imagine, I had to do much praying to maneuver through the existing style of administration and denominational worship order in that church. I often wondered why God sent me to a work that was the opposite of what I had previously known. If I had started a ministry from the beginning, it would have had a Pentecostal flavor, but without a denominational name. Some people expected me to do things exactly like it was done previously under former pastors, and I certainly understood that. As I prayed for guidance from God, He led me away from the norm of what the people were accustomed to, and subsequently, many left the church because they were unwilling to accept the changes God had ushered in. The decision to change things also didn't make me popular with the association of similar churches, but it had greater benefit to the ministry than first realized.

I'm reminded of King Solomon of Israel, successor to his father, King David, when God asked him what shall He give him and Solomon replied, "Give therefore thy servant an understanding heart to judge thy people, that I may discern between good and bad: for who is able to judge this thy so great a people?" (1 Kings 3:9). This unselfish response pleased God, who gave King Solomon not only what he asked for, but much more than he asked for, including riches. Following this model of prayer, I have also made similar requests for wisdom, even at the outset of being born-again and filled with the Holy Ghost, and long before knowing that God would call me to pastor His flock. Wisdom plays a huge part in the success of a Christian's life. Proverbs 2:10-11 says, "When wisdom entereth into thine heart, and knowledge is pleasant unto thy soul; Discretion shall preserve thee, understanding shall keep thee:" I recommend Solomon's prayer model for godly leadership for everyone called into the Christian ministry.

In December 2016, I saw a vision of church bishops parading onto a platform with cigarettes in their mouths and wearing brim hats like gangsters in a movie mob scene. I then saw one of them addressing a young pastor under him saying, "Oh, you're going to try and rebel against me? You're trying to correct me? You're coming against me? I can have you taken out just like that." As you can imagine, I was troubled by this vision. God gave me understanding of the vision; explaining that the vision is the current display of abuse of authority that has crept into the upper echelons of church leadership, where some are afraid to speak out against the conduct of certain leaders for fear of reprimand or being labelled as noncompliant. The Scripture says in 1 Peter 5:5, "Likewise, ye younger, submit yourselves unto the elder. Yea, all of you be subject one to another, and be clothed with humility: for God resisteth the proud, and giveth grace to the humble." This verse paves the way to understand how to address misconduct at leadership levels of ministry without disrespecting the position and authority of leaders, but it must be done by the leading of the Holy Spirit and with humility. *We cannot continue to close our eyes and turn our heads away from the leadership depravation and phoniness in our churches, while proclaiming normalcy.* The apostle Paul writes in 2 Corinthians 11:13-15:

> For such are false apostles, deceitful workers, transforming themselves into the apostles of Christ. And no marvel; for Satan himself is transformed into an angel of light. Therefore it is no great thing if his ministers also be transformed as the ministers of righteousness; whose end shall be according to their works.

The glory has not departed the church era as some believe. The Holy Ghost has been poured out and is still relevant in the church. However, what God has shown me is that there is a lack of leadership integrity which has minimized the visible manifestation of God's glory in some churches (not all), and it appears that the Ichabod condition is currently prevailing because of sin practices and a blatant disregard for what is right. It is a condition that lacks honor for God.

Jesus is on record in Luke 12:48 saying, ". . . For unto whomsoever much is given, of him shall be much required: and to whom men have committed much, of him they will ask the more." I therefore admonish every God-appointed bishop, pastor, administrator, and church leader to join this effort of restoring the integrity of Jesus' name back into our ministries.

Leadership integrity also involves how we as leaders promote and appoint others to ministry offices and other positions of leadership. Every church or ministry should have some form of leadership structure with authority to appoint and promote, that does not include nepotism as the sole basis for appointments and promotions, which was previously discussed in greater detail. Nepotism is based on favor granted to relatives. This is a popular yet silent activity that goes on in many churches. It is a way to keep control of a ministry within a family. The problem is that not every son or daughter, not every brother or sister, is qualified to succeed a father or mother who is pastoring or leading a ministry, nor are they always God choice's for filling key leadership positions. For those of us who are familiar with Eli the priest mentioned in 1 Samuel chapters 2-4, we remember that he allowed his two sons to defile the priestly order; how they abhorred the offering of the Lord, and laid with the women that assembled at the door of the tabernacle of the congregation. Because integrity in ministry leadership is very important, God sent a prophet to declare judgement against Eli and his two sons.

Appointments to positions of leadership, including ministerial ordinations, should not be done with secret gifts or bribery, which are things offered to induce favor or special consideration, neither should they be used as personal leverage in acts of dishonesty. Acts 8 speaks about a man named Simon who once bewitched people with sorcery but later followed the apostle Philip as a believer. Simon was amazed at how God was using Philip through miracles and signs as he was preaching in Samaria where many believed. When Peter and John joined Philip in Samaria, they laid hands on the new converts that they might receive the Holy Ghost. After seeing this powerful move of God through Peter and John and how the Holy Ghost came upon those converts, Simon offered them money to be able to do the same thing. Peter then rebuked Simon, saying, you and your money will perish together because you thought the gift of God could be bought with money (Acts 8:20).

I remember an incident when a young musician and minister joined in ministry with our church. He persistently desired to have private meetings with me prior to making a final decision to join us. He was relentless in obtaining assurance that he would be given special consideration if he joined our ministry. At one point he even asked, "What's in it for me?" As you might imagine, I did not think much of his question, but I continued to admonish and love him. After a short stay, he returned to his previous church, then later moved to another state where he died.

Integrity has always been an important feature in governing godly affairs. One of the things that displeased God concerning King Jeroboam of Israel is that the king made priests from the whole of the people of the high places, and "whosoever would, he consecrated him, and he became one of the priests of the high places" (1 Kings 13:33). For this sin, God purposed to cut off the house of Jeroboam from the face of the earth.

"The God of Israel said, the Rock of Israel spake to me,
He that ruleth over men must be just, ruling in the fear

of God"
(2 Samuel 23:3).

I say to every bishop, pastor, and overseer, this behavior will not continue without godly warning and judgment. According to 1 Peter 4:17, "For the time is come that judgment must begin at the house of God: and if it first begin at us, what shall the end be of them that obey not the gospel of God?"

Standards Integrity

Do you have a code of behavior that you live by? Is your code of behavior observed and respected by others? Are you the type of person who finds it difficult to do things considered beneath your code of conduct? If so, then you're probably a person with high conscience integrity; and doing business, ministry, or any other venture with excellence and honor is the standard you emphasize and endeavor to lift up for others to emulate. In today's society, we desperately need people who will lift up higher standards in government, business, ministry, or simply as an individual at the family reunion. There is a trend that declares everything acceptable, and as children of God, we cannot resort to these types of trends because of the effects they have on society and our fellowship with God.

Responsibility and accountability have become yokes and heavy burdens for many members of the church, and there is a doctrine that seeks to eliminate the necessity of being responsible and accountable as Christians by emphasizing grace as being sufficient in all matters of Christian conduct and living, but I beg to differ.

Quality standards of integrity should be upheld not only among Christians, but in every place where business and social activity is conducted.

Certainly, every individual will not have the same quality standards of conduct, but there are many people who consistently reflect quality of deportment in life. There is an obvious deterioration of respect that people have for each other when compared to many years ago, and that can be partly attributed to the lowering of moral standards and rejection of God in everyday life. This is not to indicate that things were perfect in society many years ago, but certainly, human relations seem to have gotten worse. There isn't a standard that is higher than the one God represents, and this is the standard that is missing. There would probably not be a "Me Too" movement if we lived with higher standards of respect toward one another. Crime, in all of its various forms, would probably not be as high if our culture was driven by qualitative standards, and families taught better moral standards to their children. Do I believe the world would be free of evil or wrongdoing if we had better standards? Absolutely not! The problems of society will always be connected to the sin which is in mankind, therefore, we must sincerely seek after God and endeavor to present standards of excellence, with Christ as our example in love, humility, forgiveness, and faith.

Every Christian establishment should uphold godly standards of ministry conduct that are scripturally inspired. The Lord speaks to the prophet Isaiah saying, "...lift up a standard for the people" (Isaiah 62:10). Everything the Bible teaches of God is standard-driven; we cannot escape these standards, but we should embrace them as God's only way of being represented to the world. As a believer, what standards of God are you teaching your children and bringing forth for the good of others? In other words, what are you doing on a regular basis as a Christian to improve yourself and those around you, be it friends, family members, coworkers, or other believers?

On a certain occasion, Jesus met with His disciples and taught them a very valuable lesson about being examples and setting a high standard of serving one another by washing His disciples feet. He said to them that, if He, their Lord and Master, washed their feet, they also should wash one another's feet. What an awesome act of humility! He also stated to them, "For I have given you an example, that ye should do as I have done to you" (John 13:15).

There is a multiplicity of areas where we can lift standards for others to follow. For example, there is a need to see fathers and mothers as not only parents, but as role models. There is a need for government officials and politicians to govern with standards of equality and excellence. Unfortunately, television has introduced into our culture so many negatives that actually tear down good standards and present things in a way that God never intended, particularly regarding relationships. What has become acceptable in many areas of life is really a disgrace to God's grace. To make matters clearer, the Bible predicted that living standards would deteriorate. The apostle Paul writes in his second letter to Timothy that in the last days, dangerous and unhealthy times would come. Men would be "lovers of their own selves, covetous, boasters, proud, blasphemers, disobedient to parents, unthankful, unholy." You can learn more about these behaviors in 2 Timothy 3:1-5, but God tells us to turn away from such traditions, even from those who endorse them and who have made them acceptable standards. As the Church, we cannot fall into these patterns and call them right.

So many ministries have compromised biblical standards to attract youth, millennials, and many other adults. Not surprisingly, the trade-off is devastating when the holy standards of God are being watered down, omitted from Sunday school curriculums, and diminished in other areas of instruction. The affects are real, causing many people to become spoiled after the philosophies and traditions of the world, and not after the true and living God.

Breaking rank with integrity may open communications with family, friends, coworkers, and others who are not committed to integrity. It may even position you to gain popularity. However, there is one thing breaking rank with integrity will never do: it will never please God. Godly integrity will be a lifestyle that repels others, or it will be a magnet that attracts others to you. Luke 6:22 states, "Blessed are ye, when men shall hate you, and when they shall separate you from their company . . ." Jesus also mentions in John 7:7, "The world cannot hate you; but me it hateth, because I testify of it, that the works thereof are evil." So, we understand that the path of integrity is not a popular one. Therefore, I say unto Christians, even as Jesus Himself has said, do not be surprised if the world hates you (1 John 3:13).

There is a teaching in churches and over social media that broadens the perceptions of the dimensions of the kingdom of heaven's gate that leads into life, as though everyone will be able to enter through this gate. On the other hand, there is a teaching that reduces the perceptions of the gate dimensions that lead into destruction, as though few people will enter through this gate. However, let's look at what Jesus says in Matthew 7:13-14:, "Enter ye in at the strait gate; for wide is the gate, and broad is the way, that leadeth to destruction, and many there be which go in thereat: Because strait is the gate, and narrow is the way, which leadeth unto life, and few there be that find it."

In the absence of integrity standards, Christ virtues are no longer esteemed and they hold no place in a person's conscience. Unlike some retail stores that remove certain items from inventory that are not selling, the church should not remove any of its divine inventory items in order to increase membership, or generate better attendance at worship services. For example, nothing in the Word of God should be altered to accommodate the wishes of the people. God says in Malachi 3:6, "For I am the LORD, I change not . . ." The writer of Hebrews also declared that Jesus Christ is the same yesterday, today, and forever (Hebrews 13:8). Therefore, the Word of God must be highly exalted in our teaching and preaching without compromise.

The least or worst executed action or application should never be the standard by which we live, nor the way the Church does its ministry.

CHAPTER NINE
Obedience Integrity

This particular integrity class is of grave importance because everything we will ever do that pleases God will involve obeying God. The Scriptures are filled with real-life illustrations that demonstrate obedience or disobedience to God, and the results of each are astronomically different. Throughout Israel's history, God has instructed the Jews to obey His voice, commandments, ordinances, and instructions. In Exodus 19, after God had delivered the Israelites out of Egyptian bondage, bringing them across the Red Sea into the Sinai desert, Moses went up the mountain and God begin speaking to him, telling him to tell the people that if they obeyed Him and keep His covenant, they would be a special treasure to Him, a peculiar people, unlike any other people; they would be a kingdom of priests and a holy nation. When Moses delivered the message, all the people responded with an emphatic yes to God's words. However, the people did not hold true to their commitment to obey; for throughout their generations they had multiple episodes of disobedience to God, even as we do today.

It is unreasonable to try and address every infraction by Israel against God's laws found in Scripture, but I will address some of them to help us understand the significance of having *obedience integrity*.

We understand that through one man's disobedience many were made sinners when Adam and Eve ate of the forbidden tree in the garden of Eden, and this alone shows the enormous damage that can be inflicted by disobeying anything God has instructed us to do. Unfortunately, each of us has come short by disobeying God in some form or another, but God is merciful and forgiving—though this does not excuse our actions of disobeying the Father.

Obedience and disobedience, both have tremendous advantage and disadvantage when interacting with God. This is particularly important in the modern age where many Christians do not see obedience to God as relevant, because many Christians rely heavily on the dispensation of God's grace for automatic forgiveness of disobedience, whereas grace is not a *statute of exemption*. It is clearly spelled out in Deuteronomy 28 how God dealt with the early Israelites under the leadership of Moses, and what was written concerning the blessings for obedience and the punishment for disobedience. The call to obedience is further extended through the Old Testament prophets. The prophet Isaiah in 1:19-20 said, "If ye be willing and obedient, ye shall eat the good of the land: but if ye refuse and rebel, ye shall be devoured with the sword: for the mouth of the Lord hath spoken it." Throughout Israel's history, the people repeatedly disobeyed God and were punished by their enemies. The kings of Israel and Judah led their respective kingdoms into idolatry and the worship of pagan gods. The kings persecuted and imprisoned God's prophets that were sent to warn them. The people adopted the ways of heathen countries while forgetting the God who delivered them and brought them into their respective lands. As a result, God sent them into captivity in Babylon. After seventy years of Babylonian captivity, God again had mercy upon His people. He stirred the spirit of Cyrus, the king of Persia, to write a proclamation for the exiles to return to Jerusalem to rebuild the temple. The book of Ezra records Zerubbabel as leader of the first group to return, followed by Ezra, and the book of Nehemiah describes the activities of Nehemiah, who led an expedition to rebuild the walls around the city of Jerusalem.

The first king of Israel was Saul of Benjamin as recorded in 1 Samuel. God was displeased with Saul because of his disobedience. The prophet Samuel came into prominence under the priestly reign of Eli and his two sons, and he was instrumental during this time as God's prophet to Israel, installing Saul as king. But, let's take a closer into Saul's fall from the kingship of Israel.

Saul's kingship appeared doomed from the outset because of the circumstances surrounding his appointment as king. During the years that Israel were being judged by various judges, the elders of Israel complained about not having a king as other countries. They went to the prophet Samuel and made their case. Samuel was displeased at the request, but he prayed about it. Probably to his surprise, God told him to listen to their request and let them have a king, but He made it clear that their whole reasoning for wanting a king was out of rejection for God's reign over them. Therefore, Samuel was to protest solemnly and let the people know the type of king who would reign over them. When reading the dreadful details in 1 Samuel 8:11-19, I think I would have reversed my request for a king after hearing what kind of king Saul was going to be. Saul, as a selfish and heartless ruler, was going to take from them, but none of that mattered to the people of Israel.

Physically, Saul was considered an attractive man, a choice young man who stood taller from his shoulders and upward than most men. He was the cream of the crop; no one being a better choice. However, God was in control of the entire selection process, so Samuel anointed him king.

Let's take a closer look at some of Saul's actions as a young king. Upon being anointed king, he was given his first assignment by the prophet Samuel, which was to meet him in a place called Gilgal to offer burnt offerings and to sacrifice peace offerings (1 Samuel 10:8). He was advised to wait there seven days, pending Samuel's arrival and further instruction. This was to be a joyous crowning of the first king of Israel. Prior to Samuel's arrival at Gilgal, Saul and Israel had a skirmish with a well-known adversary, the Philistines, and Saul's men were frightened and distressed, hiding in caves, thickets, rocks, high places, and pits. Samuel the prophet was delayed in arriving at Gilgal, and Saul's men were beginning to scatter from him, so Saul took it upon himself to offer the burnt offering and the peace offering. When he completed the sacrifices, Samuel arrived and Saul went out to meet him. Samuel, upon learning what Saul had done, was furious, telling Saul he had acted foolishly, that he should have kept the commandment to wait, that God would have established him as king over Israel forever. Because of Saul's disobedience, Samuel told him that his kingdom would not continue, that God wanted someone whose heart was after Him. This was Saul's first blunder.

Saul's second mistake is recorded in 1 Samuel 15, where again he was given an assignment by Samuel. This time he was to go to battle against Amalek, kill everything and everybody, not even sparing the sheep, oxen, camels, women, or children. The instructions seemed pretty clear, but Saul, as was his manner, disobeyed the instruction. He didn't kill the king of the Amalekites, and he saved the best sheep and oxen. Everything he considered good, he spared or kept for themselves. This seemed to have been the breaking point. When Samuel came and discovered what Saul had done, the Lord spoke to Samuel and said that He deeply regretted making Saul king. This also grieved Samuel, and he cried out to the Lord all night because of Saul's disobedience. These events turned God's heart to David, who would eventually become Saul's replacement as king, and he was one in whom God was pleased.

Obedience integrity is gravely important for the children of God in every instance. Some people will comment that obedience is not as important in post-Christ times as it was in pre-Christ dispensations, but I differ with that assessment and will explain it later. After Saul's second incident, Samuel asked him, "Hath the Lord as great delight in burnt offerings and sacrifices, as in obeying the voice of the Lord?" (1 Samuel 15:22). Samuel went on to tell Saul that to obey is better than sacrifice. What we glean from this is that whatever situation we find ourselves in, we are to keep in mind what we're supposed to do. Oftentimes as pastors and leaders, it appears that God has forgotten us because things aren't happening as quickly as we'd like, e.g., people leave our ministries, growth is stagnant, and God appears silent. My admonition is to keep doing the last known instruction until God gives another one. Too often, pastors are drawn away from their assignments and end up disobeying their ministry calls, all in an attempt to fit in and appear successful.

Here's another case of disobedience that should weigh heavily on our consciences when we are being tempted to disobey God:

During Solomon's kingship over Israel as David's successor, God determined to rend the kingdom from Solomon's son Rehoboam, giving ten tribes to Jeroboam as the consequence of Solomon's sins, but He would leave the tribe of Judah to Rehoboam for David's sake. During Jeroboam's reign as king over the ten tribes, he constructed places of idol worship as a deterrent to the people returning to Jerusalem to worship. This displeased the Lord.

As a result of Jeroboam's sin, God sent a prophet to Jeroboam to cry out against the altars of pagan worship where the people offered incense, saying, "O altar, altar, thus saith the LORD; Behold, a child shall be born unto the house of David, Josiah by name; and upon thee shall he offer the priests of the high places that burn incense upon thee, and men's bones shall be burnt upon thee" (1 Kings 13:2). The prophet was given specific instructions by God what to say during this encounter with Jeroboam. Jeroboam resented the prophet's prophesy, and extended his arm to grab the prophet, but his arm withered up, and he was unable to pull it to his body. After Jeroboam asked the prophet to pray for him, the prophet entreated God on his behalf and Jeroboam's arm was restored. Afterwards, Jeroboam asked the prophet to come home with him to refresh himself, but the prophet refused, saying, "For so was it charged me by the word of the Lord. Saying, eat no bread, nor drink water, nor turn again by the same way that thou camest" (1 Kings 13:9). However, there was an old prophet who dwelt nearby who had heard about the prophet's activity from his sons. So, he had his sons saddle his ass, and he went to meet the prophet to ask him to come home with him to dine. The younger prophet replied the same as he did to Jeroboam, but this is where the young prophet was greatly tested: the old prophet said he was also a prophet, and an angel told him to bring him back home to eat and drink, but he lied to him.

Far too many times, a younger preacher listens to an older seasoned preacher who mentors or advises the younger irresponsibly. We're often taught to obey and submit to those who are our seniors, and who are more experienced in ministry, but what if God gives a specific instruction to obey, as He did with the young prophet? The answer is not always as simple because the younger person does not want to be looked upon by the older person as disobedient. The point here is that the prophet who lied was deceitful; having selfish intent when advising the young prophet. In the church, and rightfully so, anyone considered to be at odds with established policies of governance should not be given consideration for increased responsibility. Therefore, in the situation between the two prophets, it is easy to understand the possible reasoning of the younger prophet. Regardless of the prophet's reasoning, there was still a breach of *obedience integrity*.

The younger prophet listened to the old prophet and went home with him. As they were sitting at a table eating, the older prophet prophesized the word of the Lord to the younger, saying, "Forasmuch as thou hast disobeyed the mouth of the LORD, and hast not kept the commandment which the LORD thy God commanded thee, But camest back, and hast eaten bread and drunk water in the place, of the which the LORD did say to thee, Eat no bread, and drink no water; thy carcase shall not come unto the sepulcher of thy fathers" (1 Kings 13:22). When the younger prophet departed, he was killed by a lion. People passed by and saw the lion standing over the dead carcass and told everyone in the city. When the old prophet heard about it, he knew it was the younger prophet who had come to his house to eat who was disobedient to the word of the Lord and was delivered by the Lord to the lion which killed him. How dreadful of a situation. What a stern caution to anyone not having obedience integrity. I've learned through personal experiences to adhere and obey the things God says to me to the fullest extent. To say that I've been perfect in everything would not be truthful, but I'm thankful for the grace and mercy of God.

A prophet or messenger on assignment from God should not have common interest with anyone above or beyond the scope of their assignment. Otherwise, the assignment may become compromised for personal gain, ambition, or other reason.

Another biblical favorite for teaching the consequences of obedience and disobedience is Jonah. As we know, Jonah became highly convicted of God to obey, after at first being reluctant. I believe many of us have not wanted to do a certain thing after God instructed us to do it. When stationed in California while serving in the Navy in 1989, I was dealing with a withdrawn spirit, meaning, I didn't want much exposure in church environments or settings. I just wanted to attend worship, mind my own business, and depart when it was over. I was attending a church in Los

Angeles as a young minister, and I avoided a certain place of ministry knowing what God was trying to get me to do. I found myself remaining near the back of the church to avoid being noticed, not desiring to be around other clergy. However, during a Sunday morning service I went to the men's restroom, and one of the elders followed me. He calmly rebuked me and asked why was I running from God. I tried to play dumb, but I knew it was God speaking through him. On another instance, one of the older elders cried out at me after a Sunday morning worship service, saying, "You're a leader, you are a leader!" It was as though God was really trying to tell me something. Subsequently, after completely saying yes to the Lord, I went on to become the Friday night evangelistic service minister and an assistant to my pastor. I remember preaching on a Sunday morning and the glory of God appeared all over the sanctuary. I had never seen it on that magnitude while preaching. When I finished, all I could do was go to my seat next to my pastor, who said I looked surprised at being used in that capacity, which I was. One of the elders did the altar call that brought people before the altar crying on their knees. Deliverance was being wrought by the power of God. From that experience, God began to send me to other churches to preach His Word.

One of the things that hinders a believer's state of obedience are distractions, which disrupts an individual's attention more than they do an individual's time, and sometimes both. Have you ever noticed how you can have the time to do God's will, but the mind is not well focused? When a distraction has your attention, it may consume your time and deceive you into thinking you really don't have time. We must have the ability to ignore some things if we're ever going to possess obedience integrity and avoid conflicts of interest. The things we should do for God are usually in conflict with the things we want to do for ourselves and sometimes for others. We have this propensity to make the flesh a priority, and when we do, we are never pleasing to God, as it was with the young prophet who was distracted.

It is not my intent to persuade anyone that obeying God is always easy. There are various factors that influence us towards disobedience, and not all factors are malicious. I believe that the most devoted believer has had a time in their walk with God when obedience may have been an issue, and when it is an issue, God turns it into a lesson. Obedience is often learned through some sort of suffering or chastening. Hebrews 5:8 says about Jesus, "Though he were a Son, yet learned he obedience by the things which he suffered." This is not an indictment against Jesus that He was disobedient, but it does give us a clear glimpse of how the flesh battles our will to obey. We must keep in mind that Jesus took on the form of man with a human flesh. He had not known death but had to taste it for every human in order for the believer to be freed from sin's power (Hebrews 2:9). From this we can also understand how Jesus felt when asking that the cup of death be passed from Him as he prayed to the Father shortly before being betrayed by Judas (Matthew 26:36-45). What is more significant is that Jesus concluded that it wouldn't be as His flesh willed, but as the Father willed. This is a remarkable display of obedience to a great purpose, and is how every believer should strive to respond with *obedience integrity*.

CHAPTER TEN

Unity Integrity

Unity integrity is achieved when every individual involved in a process or project has proper understanding of, respect for, and acceptance of established orders; when those orders are connected to specified goals and objectives.

U nity integrity should be an integral function of the body of Christ. It is the indispensable and fundamental characteristic of the Godhead. Everywhere in life, unity is expressed in some measure, and without it, not much of anything will ever get accomplished. Whether established with ill intent or with good intent, unity can be found everywhere.

The church is mandated to have unity, and restoring unity integrity cannot be ignored if we are going to fulfill the will of God on earth. Psalm 133:1 says, "Behold, how good and how pleasant it is for brethren to dwell together in unity." Unity simply means oneness; unanimity. The opposite would be opposition, disagreement, or dissension, which is found in many churches. Sometimes I ask myself, "How did we ever get so far apart from each other with conflicting doctrines as members of the body of Christ?" The answer may not be as simple to obtain, but one thing is for certain, we must endeavor to restore the unity integrity of His name, Jesus the Christ. Any doctrine that eliminates requirements of responding in life and to

God with integrity is a disturbingly misleading doctrine that should be banned from Christian instruction. The gospel of grace does not exempt the believer from a Christ-like integrity in any area of life. Salvation is provided by the grace of God through the shedding of blood by Jesus Christ, and this grace is accessed through faith, and not of works; sanctifying the believer. But believers are accountable to God through faith in Christ, having good works as those who are sanctified. Titus 1:15-16 says:

> Unto the pure all things are pure: but unto them that are defiled and unbelieving is nothing pure; but even their mind and conscience is defiled. They profess that they know God; but in works they deny him, being abominable, and disobedient, and unto every good work reprobate.

Furthermore, Titus 3:8 states, "This is a faithful saying, and these things I will that thou affirm constantly, that they which have believed in God might be careful to maintain good works. These things are good and profitable unto men." Our good works as believers should be witnessed by others to the glory of the Father which is in heaven, and they give credence to our confessions as children of God.

Unity is also a form of solidarity, which is a union or fellowship arising from common responsibilities, interests, objectives, or standards. Jesus prayed that we all be one, that we may also be one with God the Father through the Son. He also mentions that we be made perfect in one (John 17:20-23). Being one is a strong indicator of the presence of Christ within us, and certainly something the world must see from the Church. If we are going to accurately represent unity integrity, we must obey God as sheep of God's fold. In John 10:16 Jesus said, "And other sheep I have, which are not of this fold: them also I must bring, and they shall hear my voice; and there shall be one fold, and one shepherd." I believe Jesus was speaking prophetically when referring to other sheep, recognizing a day when the Gentiles would be grafted in. We understand that Jesus came first to the Jew, and because of their unbelief, the Gentiles received grace for salvation. But on the day when Christ returns for the Church, He is coming for the sheep, those who hear His voice and obey; not for Jews only, not for Gentiles only, not for certain Church denominations, not for certain ethnicities, but for all people who are redeemed and made one by the blood of Jesus.

Paul writes in 1 Corinthians 1:10, "Now I beseech you, brethren, by the name of our Lord Jesus Christ, that ye all speak the same thing, and that there be no divisions among you; but that ye be perfectly joined together in the same mind and in the same judgment." Paul wrote this to address the contention among believers at Corinth as reported by the house of Chloe. Some would probably call the members of the house of Chloe whistle blowers, but we cannot sit idly allowing contentious and divisive behaviors in the body of Christ. Paul even asked them in 1 Corinthians 1:13, "Is Christ divided? Was Paul crucified for you? Or were ye baptized in the name of Paul?" It is important to ask these questions because there are many believers who accentuate the personalities of certain people above that of Jesus Christ, so Paul is addressing this problem with the converts at Corinth.

As I mentioned earlier regarding gift integrity, *skills, gifts, and talents in the Church must be integrated into a system designed for cohesive functionality.* Though there are differences in operation, we must walk in unity with other members with different gifts. Jealousy is common among many gifted and talented members, but we should put this away. We should never put ourselves, nor our gifts, above the *system of cohesive functionality.*

Unity has always been a quality of people working together. At one time, the whole earth spoke the same language. The people decided to build a city with a tower to make a name for themselves, so they said one to another, "Go to, let us make brick, and burn them thoroughly. And they had brick for stone, and slime had they for morter" (Genesis 11:3). When God saw how the work had progressed, He said, "... Behold, the people is one, and they have all one language; and this they begin to do: and now nothing will be restrained from them, which they have imagined to do" (Genesis 11:6). There are some key points in God's observation of the people. Firstly, the people were one. Secondly, nothing was restrained from them. What an amazing principle! How can we not understand this as the body of Christ? Well, the Lord disrupted them from building the city and tower by confounding their language and scattering them all over the earth. Babel is the name given to this place, which means *confusion* in Hebrew (Genesis 11:7-9). This might explain the various ethnicities and language barriers that exist today.

Amos 3:3 says, "Can two walk together, except they be agreed?" Here we continue to see the significance of unity integrity. *Unity can also be considered as unreserved agreements.*

Every cooperative is effective and highly impactful when there is unreserved agreement.

Unreserved means uninhibited and unrestricted. Have you ever tried to achieve something with someone who is invariably against what you're trying to achieve with them? Whether in business, government, marriage, or in ministry, walking together requires complete agreement, which is important for achieving desired outcomes.

Then there is something I call *value mismatches*. A value mismatch is a condition that exist when one or more parties do not agree because of how they value a thing. This will also hinder unity. For example, all of the people involved in the construction of the Tower of Babel had the same or similar values concerning building the tower. They apparently agreed upon its value and benefits to them. Most conflicts and disagreements will occur when a faction of a group has a value mismatch with the objective or goal. A subjective analysis will interfere with unreserved agreement, whereas an objective analysis will cause a more unified result when members of a group are trying to agree upon a course of action.

> *The sum of a thing is often determined*
> *by the representation of its values.*

Another application for unity integrity is marriage. When being questioned about divorce, Jesus said in Matthew 19:6, "Wherefore they are no more twain, but one flesh. What therefore

God hath joined together, let not man put asunder." *Asunder* in Greek means to separate, divide, or part. God intended for man and woman to have unity integrity when joined together as husband and wife.

There will always be challenges in marriage, but the husband and wife should always endeavor to keep unity integrity through every challenge. Too often, husbands and wives allow themselves to be pitted against each other for various reasons, especially when complaining to someone about the other. I've learned that everyone can't mediate a marital dispute without having some form of bias. Family members on either side are not always the best choices for mediation. Therefore, I suggest that couples seek a neutral counselor or mediator, someone unfamiliar with both individuals—but only when absolutely necessary. Couples must confront everything together with unreserved agreement to maintain marriage unity.

God puts an emphasis on the members of the church of Jesus Christ being unified in every purpose. Every outcome ever achieved collectively by the children of God occurred because they were in one accord during the process and God gave them grace. On the contrary, when they were not in one accord, the outcomes were reversed. In one particular instance, Moses sent twelve men from every tribe of Israel to spy on the land of Canaan and see the people who dwelt there, and what the land was like. After forty days of spying the land, the tribal leaders were not in agreement of their assessment of whether to go up and possess the land, or not go up. Ten of the spies elected not to go up because the people were great in number, the cities were walled, giants occupied the land, and the people were stronger. However, Caleb and Joshua took a different perspective and desired to go up immediately, believing they were well able to conquer the land. Both sides did agree that the land was good. Nevertheless, the people of Israel became afraid and were divided because of the report of the ten spies, some even desiring to return to Egypt. They murmured against God, and God was angered. As a result, God said that those who came out of the Egyptian bondage, who saw His glory and miracles in the wilderness, tempted Him ten times, and would not listen to His voice, they would not see the land promised them because they had provoked him to anger, except for Joshua and Caleb. God therefore sent the people wandering in the wilderness for forty years, a year for each day they spied the land, to die and be consumed (Numbers 13-14).

There have been occurrences in churches where congregations were split over leadership decisions. This type of situation usually causes people to leave their church to attend other churches, while the faithful endure and remain loyal until things are improved. A church with divided leadership and a fragmented congregation is unhealthy, is not postured to effectively minister to souls, and is limited in carrying out its purpose and mission. When deacons, finance workers, and board members are divided against pastors, or when ministries within a church are not cohesively joined together, the church is divided, and God is not pleased. All dissension in a church must be prayerfully addressed, with forgiveness among members, and its commitment to purpose and mission be renewed through the Holy Spirit.

When Jesus was accused of casting out devils by the power of the prince of the devils, He said to the scribes in a parable, "How can Satan cast out Satan? And if a kingdom is divided against itself, that kingdom cannot stand. And if a house be divided against itself, that house cannot stand" (Mark 3:22-25).

Being in one accord worked favorably for the disciples in the upper room on the day of Pentecost. Acts 2:1 says, "And when the day of Pentecost was fully come, they were all with one accord in one place." They were previously instructed by Christ to tarry in the city of Jerusalem until they were endued with power from on high (Luke 24:49). This refers to the promise of the Holy Ghost who Jesus said would be sent after His departure. Their schedule of daily activities while in Jerusalem leading up to the day of Pentecost is not recorded in Scripture, but it is certain they met together for prayer and fellowship. After being filled with the Holy Ghost, the disciples continued daily with one accord in the temple and breaking bread from house to house (Acts 2:46). Signs and wonders accompanied the apostles, who were in one accord. Paul writes in Philippians 2:2, "Fulfil ye my joy, that ye be likeminded, having the same love, being of one accord, of one mind."

Christ is calling the members of the body of Christ to *unity integrity* with unreserved agreement with Him and with each other in doing the will of the Father. Jesus said in Matthew 18:19, "Again I say unto you, that if two of you shall agree on earth as touching anything that they shall ask, it shall be done for them of my Father which is in heaven." As we can see, there is tremendous upside to having unity integrity, which is a champion to our success as members of the body of Christ.

CHAPTER ELEVEN
Restoring the Family

The most significant component in God's creation of life is the family. Everything born is usually considered part of some family. Family is a basic social unit that has historically consisted of one or two parents and children who live in the same household. *Family* also means the descendants of a common progenitor, which is a biologically-related ancestor. Nothing in this chapter is tailored to fit every possible scenario or situation we encounter as families. There is no one size fits all in how each of us naturally should interact as family for it to be happy and functional. There are many ministers of the gospel and various authors of books and articles who have written about how to have a successful family and marriage. We must understand that not every man or woman is the same, and as Christians we must seek to know God's will in principle and application. No marriage is naturally perfect, because as humans we are imperfect, but we must learn to overcome our differences and grow into the people we desire to be. I will not say that problems and challenges won't occur, even if you're a Christian. My sole motivation and goal is to provide spiritual insights on restoring the family integrity that has been lost or diminished, which could be a major contributing cause of dysfunction in society, even in many Christian homes and churches. It does not matter to me if a family goes out for dinner five nights a week or two nights a week to keep everyone happy and together. What I have learned is that what may work for one family may not work for another family. I do believe, however, that what God suggests to us in His Word is the right approach for every family.

Families are mentioned throughout Scripture, even as they are mentioned in today's society. However, it must be clearly understood that God designed the family, but that design has been replaced by something different to people all over the world by Satan. As a minister of the gospel, I have the responsibility of expressing this topic from a biblical perspective as God intended it, and every Christian should share this position. It is no surprise that the fabric of the family has deteriorated over the years; therefore, this chapter is committed to restoring *Family Integrity*.

The book of Genesis clearly outlines the creation of man as male and female. Man is synonymous with the word *adam* in the Hebrew, meaning man, mankind, first man, human being. According to Genesis 2:7, "And the LORD God formed man of the dust of the ground, and breathed into his nostrils the breath of life; and man became a living soul." Genesis 1:27 says, "So God created man in his own image, in the image of God created he him; male and female created he them." It is clear that God initially formed two genders as representatives of the first family of creation which were to multiply humans on earth by having offspring. The woman was created from the rib of Adam as he slept. She was brought to him by God. Upon seeing the woman, Adam named her *woman* because she was taken out of man, saying, "... This is now bone of my bones, and flesh of my flesh ..." (Genesis 2:23). From this creative process, the first family was formed.

I pen this chapter having regrets for the many mistakes I've made as a man, husband, and father. I first married at the age of 27, and lacked the insight that I now have, and subsequently, my marriage failed. Then I married the second time 21 years later. During my first marriage I did not have a full grasp of my role as a husband and father as I probably should have. And as it is with many young men getting married, we often think we know more than we actually do. My mother and father divorced when I was very young, so I did not always have the advantage of a father as a role model to teach me how to be a good husband and father. My mother later remarried, but the relationship between my step-father and I was not always good in my childhood; it improved when I became an adult and God saved me.

We went to church religiously not knowing God, and I never heard specific, subject-matter teachings on marriage, finance, or other necessary life-related topics. Most of what the preachers preached was tailored around making the congregation emotionally excited. A large misconception among many people is that being a good Christian translates into being good husbands and wives. What we are in designation as spouses and parents must be accurately understood and applied.

There is no one best place to find a spouse. As a Christian, the place to meet a spouse is not always in the same church, and just because someone confesses the Christian faith is no assurance that you'll be happy with them. Two Christian partners should have compatibilities beyond their faith to be truly compatible with each other. As you'll read later in the dating section, sex should not be a precondition in any Christian marriage. For the married, would you have married your spouse had you not had sex with them? This is not to insinuate that there are no Christian couples who refrained from sex prior to marriage; there are many. My marriage to my second wife was without premarital sex because we wanted to glorify God in our bodies and respect each other. For the Christian couple, both individuals should have a place in the heart for each other, and a place in the heart where God is jointly worshipped.

There is no counsel that can make two people with different living philosophies happy together in marriage unless compromise is made. Philosophy is a system of principles for guidance in practical affairs. Married couples usually get married to be happy with the person they've married, and certainly, there are those who marry for other reasons. I've learned that love is not the single counsel or solution for having a peaceful and harmonious marriage when everything outside of love is broken, e.g., communication. There is one sure way to have a happy marriage, and that's to marry the right person. Someone might ask, "How do you determine who is right to marry?" There is no single correct response for that question because everyone is different, and that's why dating is important. It is rare and extremely unusual for God to advise anyone who to marry, and the marriage of Joseph and Mary is one of those situations. However, there are situations when God might warn against marrying a particular person. Sometimes those warning come from parents, friends, or other persons with unselfish motives. But for sure, you'll know after getting married to them if they were the right choice. Marriage, like making a house purchase or other large investment, requires thoughtful consideration before saying "I do." Not every good person, not every ministry worker, not every person who regularly attends church will always be the right person to marry.

There is much deserved attention given to spouses who were victims of some form of abuse in a home. However, there are children who were not the targets of abuse, but suffered from the effects of being in a home where spouses abused each other, and were exposed to a negative environment. When a child is exposed to negativity in a home; when they do not understand why dad or mom is hardly around or comes home intoxicated; when they observe mothers and fathers sleeping in separate bedrooms; when they constantly hear derogatory exchanges between mom and dad; when children witness a single parent with different sexual partners in the home, and when they witness pushing and shoving without understanding the reasons why, it is likely that some of these behaviors will be adopted by the child when he or she becomes an adult. When these types of occurrences are in the home, family integrity is lacking. Certainly, there are many other situations that I didn't mention that have equally destructive effects on the fabric of the family, such as marriage infidelity. Regardless of the causes and who is at fault, we must take comprehensive measures to restore the integrity of what Jesus intended for the family, especially in the face of a world reeling aimlessly out of moral control. Our society is strengthened and enhanced by the Christ values taught and expressed within the family.

The Man

God established a precedent for man from the beginning when He stated that a man should leave his father and mother, and cleave, which literally means to be joined to his wife (Genesis 2:24). It would appear to some people that Adam did not stay close enough to Eve after he received God's instructions saying, "But of the fruit of the tree which is in the midst of the garden, God hath said, Ye shall not eat of it, neither shall ye touch it, lest ye die" (Genesis 3:3); giving the serpent ample opportunity to make his impression on her with a bunch of lies that cost them both expulsion from the Garden of Eden.

It is important to note that the man, Adam, is called the husband of Eve, and she is now called his wife, as noted in the aforementioned Scripture. It is also interesting to note that neither had a childhood. They did not have parental guidance to instruct, guide, or chasten them in a maturating process as children; they only had God's instructions. They are designated not just male and female, but also husband and wife. This is first mentioned in Genesis 3:6 where the woman took of the fruit of the forbidden tree, ate it, and also gave some to her husband, who also ate it. It appears that nothing happened until the man ate, and then their eyes were both opened and they realized they were naked. God had given instruction to the man concerning the trees, but Satan, the serpent, beguiled Eve and persuaded her that God was not telling the truth. Unfortunately, she believed the serpent.

Seeing that the man is husband to the woman, God instructs him to love his wife. There is always a question as to how men are to love their wives, and I've discovered that natural love expressions will vary from man to man, because not only are men different, women are also different. There is no universal way that a single man can express love to any woman and get the same results or response. For example, there are some pharmaceutical prescriptions that have negative side effects on some people but no side effects on others, or there are some pharmaceutical prescriptions that are designed for a certain condition that may not work well on every individual with the same condition.

Many men describe love as giving the woman everything she asks for, regardless of how it is obtained. Their goal is to make and keep her happy. Some men might love this way, but I would not endorse this type behavior for several reasons. Love for each other should not be material-based, and many husbands have drowned themselves in financial debt to keep a wife happy. Ephesians 5:25-28 tells the husband to love his wife as Christ loved the Church and gave himself for it. God does not give us everything we ask for, and I'm glad He doesn't. Therefore, husbands should not interpret loving their wives any differently. The Scripture points out that, as husbands love their own bodies, so are they to love their wives. For example, a husband might exercise and care for his body for various health reasons, and he may desire that his wife share in the same self-care by encouraging her to participate likewise. There are many things God admonishes us to do because He loves us, but we sometimes ignore or don't respond to Him as we should.

Another point of consideration is that of the husband's leadership of his family, particularly in critical times, and not leaving the wife to face difficulties alone. Paul writes in 1 Corinthians 11:3 that "... the head of every man is Christ; and the head of the woman is the man; ..." Husbands are to comfort their wives, encourage them, and bear them up in the strength of the Lord. 1 Peter 3:7 admonishes husbands to not lead their wives emotionally, but according to knowledge. He is to respect his wife as being the weaker of the two of them, but joint-heirs of God's blessing through grace. Doing this prevents the husband's prayers from being obstructed. In other words, husbands should live, reason, and interact with their wives according to the revelation of God and His will for the family, not according to the world. It's important for the husband to approach his family roles positively and confidently, otherwise his roles as husband and father may not be effective to other family members.

When the husband and wife have bonded spirits and have mutual respect in the marriage; when they're open to discuss their differences about life and family without their differences becoming partitions in the marriage; when they both love and fear the Lord, respecting His Holy Word, then they give themselves a great opportunity of having a successful marriage.

Colossians 3:19 says, "Husbands, love your wives, and be not bitter against them." Some wives tend to create situations for their husbands to feel bitter against them. It is probable that Adam felt bitter toward Eve when he said to God, ". . . The woman whom thou gavest to be with me, she gave me of the tree, and I did eat" (Genesis 3:12). This is an area where husbands must be strong as the head of households. A man must understand that the woman has a different design and will not always see or respond to things as he typically would, even though she is made from him; therefore, the husband who is unaware of this truth may find himself constantly feeling bitter over things his wife does. Bitterness left without proper attention is devastating to both parties. In some situations, a wife may become as a boxer's punching bag when the object of her husband's frustration is aimed toward her, and no one wins when domestic violence enters a marriage. There are other negative reactions husbands can have when bitter toward their wives; therefore, I say to husbands, quickly recognize when you're bitter, pray to God, have the necessary discussions with your wife, and avoid coming apart at the seams over any conflict while working towards a resolution.

The Woman

Now, let's begin a discussion about the woman; let's examine her design and role in light of Scripture. When Adam and Eve sinned in the Garden of Eden, they hid themselves from God after recognizing they were naked. Subsequently, God made them aprons to cover themselves before passing judgment on their disobedience. Genesis 3:16 says, "Unto the woman he said, I will greatly multiple thy sorrow and thy conception; in sorrow thou shalt bring forth children; and thy desire shall be to thy husband, and he shall rule over thee." The latter part of this Scripture, "*he shall rule over thee,*" is a controversial position for many wives as it relates to their role with her husbands. For many wives it presents a great challenge for them, and consequently, many of them become aggressively resistant to this notion of submission. Many Christian wives express the opinion of unbelieving women who do not fully understand or support this scriptural position as a wife. "*He shall rule over thee*" is an often misunderstood and misapplied phrase. The result could mean a breakdown of integrity in the marriage. There are many countries where marriages are governed by their unique culture; the role of the male and female are specifically defined. However, in many Christian and non-Christian marriages, the roles of males and females will vary based on individual strengths and weaknesses in performing certain tasks, such as handling household finances, but those roles should never conflict with how God orders the family.

Let's examine what "*thy desire shall be towards they husband*" means to the wife. The word *desire* in the Hebrew text means stretching out after; longing. When considering the man's role to love and cleave to his wife, how marvelous it is to see her stretching out and longing for her husband in a congruent manner.

On the issue of *ruling over*, it's not about who has the most control in the marriage, because husbands and wives usually have shared responsibilities rearing the children, maintaining the finances, home care, and other family-related matters. There is a spirit that seeks to undermine the woman's response to her husband by making her feel threatened by an assumption that she must be a subordinate or inferior partner in the marriage. This is a lie. This has nothing to do with women's rights or any other subject of contention regarding women that is often argued about in society. This is a matter solely between a husband and wife. The devil desires to put animosity between the man and woman, which is not God's will, and by doing so, he corrupts the integrity of the marriage. Unfortunately, there are some women who don't believe they should live subserviently because it makes them feel second-rate to their husbands, and some vow never to marry for this reason. It is clear throughout Scripture that God intended for man to have a more decisive role in the marriage, and this is not male chauvinism; it is the will of God.

It is difficult for some women to accept the role of submission, but wives are to submit to their own husbands because it is the proper thing to do according to Scripture (Colossians 3:18). I have conversed with many wives who either feel their husbands are not converted, don't know enough, or simply aren't good enough leaders of the family for them to submit to. Many Christian wives try hard to please God but often struggle in this one area, regularly praying for God's help in their lives. I don't have an answer for wives who live under these conditions other than to keep praying, don't become weary in well-doing, and hope in God's grace. Submission is the recommended Scriptural response for the woman in marriage, but in the modern era of women's rights, many women are inspired to be more independent. The apostle Peter writes in 1 Peter 3:1, "Likewise, ye wives, be in subjection to your own husbands; that, if any obey not the word, they also may without the word be won by the conversation of the wives;"

What Peter is communicating to the wife is the manner in which godly women should conduct themselves with their husbands, especially when he has not yet received Christ; not condemning him, but being a godly example before him through subjection as his wife.

A woman's subjection to her husband does not mean she should obey and follow insane and unlawful instructions he demands of her, but lawful and righteous applications should be factored into interpreting and understanding this Scripture.

When a wife has a desire for her husband to be saved, it is important to pray for him and live a virtuous life before him in love. Proverbs 31:10-31 gives an astonishing blueprint of a virtuous woman. There are some who do not consider Scriptures concerning marriage and family relations as a reliable source for shaping family values. Many unbelievers consider the Bible an antiquated and old-fashioned way to govern a home, and out of touch with the trends and challenges facing the present-day family. However, as Christians, we must not abandon God's word, but continually uphold it as not only reliable, but the relevant, true, and perfect source for structuring and modeling the family after God's will.

Dating Integrity

Dating integrity is understood from the observation of Christian virtues for the Christian. For many, those virtues are learned early when youth participate in Sunday school and other Christ-related learning programs. They are also learned from fathers and mothers in the home, and carried over into the dating experience when the children are older.

The first building block used in establishing a dating relationship should be respect. *Dating is a process of getting to know someone.* Rarely will two people marry each other without spending time interacting with each other and discussing various life topics. These interactions and discussions will usually determine if a dating process will lead to something long-term, such as marriage, or end with both individuals going their separate way. Respect for each other must be a factor in dating because neither person wants to be disrespected in the dating process. Respect is also an expression of honoring someone; it is not discourteous. I have heard people generally say that, "If a person does not respect his or herself, neither will others respect them." There are some relationships where two people do no treat each other with civility. Therefore, if two people are going to have dating integrity, respect must be given to each other.

One of the major violations of dating integrity among Christians is sex prior to marriage. I realize this is a hot topic, but it is one that requires more discussion. Fornication is voluntary intercourse between two unmarried persons or two persons not married to each other. Sex before marriage is becoming more acceptable because the subject is rarely mentioned, even in many churches. Regardless of the mistakes you and I have made as Christians or as unsaved people, we must embrace these virtues even while our society abandons them. I feel confident saying that many Christian men and women have indulged in premarital sex prior to marriage. When dating, couples usually fuel the flames of sexual desire with excessive kissing and touching, and when that happens, it increases the possibility of sexual intercourse occurring.

The question is, what did God intend as the premarital standard? Because grace abounds, should we continue the act of fornication before marriage? The answer is simple for the Christian and can be found throughout New Testament Scriptures. For instance, 1 Corinthians 6:18 says, "Flee fornication. Every sin that a man doeth is without the body; but he that committeth fornication sinneth against his own body." Television and social media has infiltrated the airways presenting fornication as acceptable in our society and part of the normal response between part-ners, whether as heterosexual, bisexual, or homosexual. Any stance against sexual immorality is considered self-righteous and out of touch with reality. However, there is a significant mandate to the Church to not compromise godly teachings about sexual relations and marriage.

The apostle Paul writes in Romans 1:18-19, "For the wrath of God is revealed from heaven against all ungodliness and unrighteousness of men, who hold the truth in unrighteousness; Because that which may be known of God is manifest in them; for God hath shewed it unto them." Paul goes on to say in Romans 1:26-27:

> For this cause God gave them up unto vile affections: for even their women did change the natural use into that which is against nature: And likewise also the men, leaving the natural use of the woman, burned in their lust one toward another; men with men working that which is unseemly, and receiving in themselves that recompense of their error which was meet.

We must not forget that God destroyed Sodom and Gomorrah for acts of homosexuality (Genesis 18-19). In Leviticus 20:13, it is written, "If a man also lie with mankind, as he lieth with a woman, both of them have committed an abomination: they shall surely be put to death; their blood shall be upon them." Some people argue that the Old Testament laws given by Moses to Israel are irrelevant in the dispensation of grace given through Jesus Christ, and therefore gives acceptance for acts of homo-sexuality. However, I would like to point out that God has not changed His attitude concerning sin. Malachi 3:6 says, "For I am God, I change not; . . . We may not be able to change the fact that sexual immorality is integrated in society, but we can conclude that its root cause is sin. If homosexuality was a sin in the Old

Testament, it is sin in the New Testament. The good news is that there is forgiveness with God for all sins.

The apostle Paul writes in 1 Corinthians 7:1-2, "Now concerning the things whereof ye wrote unto me: It is good for a man not to touch a woman. Nevertheless, to avoid fornication, let every man have his own wife, and let every woman have her own husband." I am challenging every Christian to commit to restoring dating integrity with Christian values.

There is a fear among some people of getting married and being disappointed if sexual pleasure is missing. The right formula for sexual pleasure in Christian marriage is a subject reserved for the husband and wife. Marrying for sex only is considered by many to be a good strategy for long-term happiness, but there are other things to consider for having a happy marriage that will vary with different couples. Believers are to trust God when considering marriage. Hebrews 13:4 says, "Marriage is honorable in all, and the bed undefiled: but whoremongers and adulterers God will judge."

Fornication is not a prerequisite for marriage, and parents should teach their teenage children the ways of the Lord as they enter courtship years.

Another feature of dating integrity is the complete transparency of both individuals. It could be devastating if a partner conceals negative and damaging information about themselves that is later revealed in the marriage. This could sever trust in a marriage and eventually lead to separation. When a Christian decides to abstain from sex before marriage, there should be discussions of individual sexuality between persons contemplating marriage. There should also be discussions concerning having children to determine if both parties have agreement.

The church must take an aggressive stand against the world's definition of family. *The church of Jesus Christ should not bow to same-sex marriage ideologies or ungodly concepts of family.* Joshua, when leading the people of Israel to their promised land of occupancy made this statement:

> And if it seems evil unto you to serve the LORD, choose you this day whom ye will serve; whether the gods which your fathers served that were on the other side of the flood, or the gods of the Amorites, in whose land ye dwell: but as for me and my house, we will serve the LORD (Joshua 24:15).

The Final Word

Every behavior is the reciprocal characteristic of who is being represented.

Having integrity does not imply living a perfect life. It is a manner of addressing the ill's affecting every part of life; it is a way of doing damage control on damaging personal behaviors, correcting erroneous thinking patterns, and ultimately restoring the integrity of Jesus' name back into the conversation of daily lives. Integrity houses good values, intentions, behaviors, and works. The Word of God, through the Holy Spirit's indwelling presence, is the only standard for governing the body of Christ, and any deviation from this influence will introduce compromise of the things God intended. From a Christian's perspective, the purest way of restoring the integrity of His name is through conscience integrity that leads to obedience to God. As the writer of the book of Ecclesiastes has said, "Let us hear the conclusion of the whole matter: Fear God, and keep his commandments: for this is the whole duty of man" (Ecclesiastes 12:13).

Father God, let every reader be inspired and blessed by the contents of this book which I have obeyed your instruction to write. As born-again believers who are Holy Ghost filled, grant us an unwavering fortitude to stand against the wiles of the devil aimed at defaming the name of JESUS and against all efforts designed to destroy Christian integrity. Lord, grant us the wisdom, knowledge, and strength through your grace to persevere through the trials we encounter in spreading the gospel of Christ. Let us not as your Church falter or faint during times of societal injustice, indifference, trouble, and difficulty. Let us not diminish our roles as parents, husbands, and wives, nor as Church and ministry leaders and believers in general. Father, I thank you for your abounding grace, that we, having sufficiency in all things, may abound to every good work. Help us to love one another, even as you have loved us, that our joint efforts to reach the unsaved, to minister to the saints, and to present this glorious gospel across various platforms is not a divisive work, but a unified and collaborative work pleasing in your sight. Bless the churches of the Lord Jesus Christ that preach and teach according to Scripture without compromise. All of these things do I ask in the name of Jesus Christ. Amen. ~